The Caregiver's Legal Guide to

Planning for a Loved One

with Chronic Illness

Insider Strategies to Plan for Medicaid, Veterans Benefits and Long-term Care

Christopher J. Berry, J.D., CELA

VA ACCREDITED ATTORNEY | CERTIFIED ELDER LAW ATTORNEY

Published by Advantage, Charleston, South Carolina.
Member of Advantage Media Group.

ADVANTAGE is a registered trademark and the Advantage colophon is a trademark of Advantage Media Group, Inc.

Printed in the United States of America.

ISBN: 978-1-59932-418-0
LCCN: 2014940656

Cover design by George Stevens.

Advantage Media Group is proud to be a part of the Tree Neutral® program. Tree Neutral offsets the number of trees consumed in the production and printing of this book by taking proactive steps such as planting trees in direct proportion to the number of trees used to print books. To learn more about Tree Neutral, please visit **www.treeneutral.com**. To learn more about Advantage's commitment to being a responsible steward of the environment, please visit **www.advantagefamily.com/green**

Advantage Media Group is a publisher of business, self-improvement, and professional development books and online learning. We help entrepreneurs, business leaders, and professionals share their Stories, Passion, and Knowledge to help others Learn & Grow. Do you have a manuscript or book idea that you would like us to consider for publishing? Please visit **advantagefamily.com** or call **1.866.775.1696**.

The Caregiver's Legal Guide to

Planning for a Loved One

with Chronic Illness

I'd like to dedicate this book to my wonderful family.

Thank you to my parents, Jim & Laurie Berry. The best, most supportive parents that I could ask for. Thank you. Without your support and unconditional love, I would not be the person who I am today.

My wonderful children, Ryan & Madison. You are the reason I work so hard. You both are the lights of my life, my purpose. A smile or hug from one of you is by far the best thing that can happen to me in a day.

Rochelle, thank you for coming in to my life, I could not ask for a better, more supportive and loving partner.

I am blessed in so many ways.

Without my loving family, this book would not have happened. Thank you.

CONTENTS

INTRODUCTION

In its 2004 national survey, the American Association of Retired Persons, more commonly known as AARP, found that more than 44 million Americans provide care to an adult without payment for their services. Maybe you are one of those 44 million. The road of a caregiver is fraught with potholes, wrong turns, and stress. Let's also not forget about all of the bad advice out there, including bad legal advice. As a Certified Elder Law Attorney, which is the top designation someone in my profession can earn, I have heard all kinds of stories that start with "My neighbor said we should do this," or "My financial planner said to do this."

This book is your guidebook for the elder care journey. If you are caring for a loved one who has a chronic illness or is facing the frailties of aging, this book may be the most important legal book you pick up. The knowledge you'll gain and the strategies you'll find in this book will be a beacon in the night, a ray of hope as you navigate the murky waters of the elder care journey.

It is an honor and a privilege to be an elder law attorney, and I take the honor very seriously.

So who am I and why do I practice elder law? I started off in law school looking to get into a corporate concentration. I knew right off the bat that I did not want to be the typical courtroom attorney or criminal attorney. I had spent one summer at the

Wayne County prosecutor's office in Detroit and that experience taught me exactly what I did not want to do. I was in the major drug unit, where we put major criminals behind bars. I thought it was important and necessary work, but it really was not fulfilling for me because I was surrounded by people I would not bring home to meet my family. I knew very shortly into that assignment that my personality was not confrontational, and that I did not want to be that attorney on *Law & Order*.

So I was looking for a way that I could help, but I wanted to work with good people, responsible people, whom I would feel comfortable about bringing home to meet my family. It all worked out as I visualized it because, in reality, my clients are like family. We get to know each other and we learn things about each other's families. They learn about my young children and I learn about the various people in their families. So what I do is very different from what your typical courtroom attorney, your generalized stereotypical attorney, does.

After my stint in the Wayne County prosecutor's office, although I knew exactly what I did not want to do, I was not sure of exactly what I did want to do. As soon as I graduated from law school, I took a job reviewing contracts for a corporation. The pay was great and I did it for a year, but eventually, I determined that that work was not very fulfilling either. So I joined a small firm where I was able, basically, to pick the practice area I wanted to get into, and I chose to get involved in estate planning. Estate planning law would allow me to work with good families, and that was important to me. Also, I would not have to worry about opposing counsel or judges, and I was able to control my calendar and my schedule, so if I wanted to take time off to go to my son's soccer practice, I would be able to do that. It also was an area of law where I could use my undergraduate background and training in finance and psychology. I knew I would really be able to help people and their families and felt that I could do some good in the world. My decision had been made, validated, and solidified! What a great feeling it is to know what your life's work should be, to know what you truly want to do and to be confident that you can do a really great job at it.

I started out at a small firm doing estate planning but eventually founded my own firm, The Elder Care Firm, with the mission of helping Michigan families protect what they've earned to preserve what they value. Today our firm is growing, with offices in Brighton, Livonia, and throughout the surrounding Metro-Detroit area.

When I first started practicing, I was bombarded with clients calling to say their mother had been diagnosed with dementia or their spouse had fallen and broken a hip and was being discharged. They all had the same question: "What do we do now?" At first I didn't know how to help them. So I did my homework, researched the issues, and became well versed in something called elder law or, as I now call it, LifeCare Planning. Eventually, I was able to help families facing the issues of long-term care, and today it is the core of my practice.

Typically, elder law attorneys focus only on the practice of moving assets around to best suit their clients' needs. That approach can be effective, up to a point. Unfortunately, it is only one small piece of the overall puzzle. Our approach is more holistic than that. We focus on life care planning, which is the holistic approach to elder law. We cover all aspects of elder law, not just the financial aspects of it. I have made elder law my focus for the past couple of years, and I am one of only a handful of Certified Elder Law Attorneys in all of Michigan. I have been ranked Superb by Avvo, which is an unbiased national ranking system for attorneys, and I have received a rating of 10 out of 10. I have been selected as a top lawyer for estate planning in elder law by *DBusiness* magazine and *Best Lawyers of America*. In 2007 I won the Spirit of Detroit Award for the community work I was doing in the metro Detroit community.

Throughout my career I have sat on numerous boards, including the Easter Seals of Michigan, and Presbyterian Villages of Michigan. I am also heavily involved with the Alzheimer's Association, and I have offered numerous presentations and continued education for social workers and financial professionals. I am also an adjunct professor of law and teach elder law to law students. But of all of that, probably the most important designation I have received is that of Certified Elder Law Attorney.

So, what is a Certified Elder Law Attorney? A Certified Elder Law Attorney is more than just an attorney who specializes in the field of elder law. A Certified Elder Law Attorney serves the interest of older and maturing populations and must meet strict, comprehensive requirements, including practicing elder law for five years before earning certification. We also must be peer-reviewed and are required to pass a day-long examination. This designation has been in existence since 1993 and I am (at the time of this writing) one of only 15 Certified Elder Law Attorneys in the entire state of Michigan and just one of only a handful in southeast Michigan.

I am one of the youngest attorneys ever to achieve the designation of Certified Elder Law Attorney. Reaching the summit of technical knowledge in my profession at such a young age makes me very proud. I continue to learn and grow daily as a Certified Elder Law Attorney. My clients enjoy great peace of mind, knowing that they are working with an expert who will be there for them and their family when they need assistance. Being a successful Certified Elder Law Attorney requires a great deal of very specialized knowledge, but it also requires a great deal of empathy and compassion.

CHAPTER ONE

The Story of Bill and Judy

As an elder law attorney, I give presentations to a great many local groups. I often talk to Alzheimer's support groups and dementia support groups. One day, my elder care coordinator received a call from a woman named Judy, who had heard me give a presentation at an Alzheimer's conference. She was concerned for her husband Bill, for whom she was caring. So she set up an appointment to come into our office and have a talk.

Judy was 65 years of age at the time. She came into my office and sat down, and I could tell right away that she was concerned and stressed, that she had a lot on her mind. Her husband was not able to make it to the meeting because, at the time, he was suffering from Alzheimer's and dementia, and she did not want to bring him along. So she left him for the day with a home care provider, someone to watch him and make sure he did not wander or hurt himself.

Judy and I sat down and we started talking about her situation. She had been caring for her husband for a number of years by then. Because of his worsening Alzheimer's disease, he was becoming more difficult to care for. He was 10 years older than Judy—75 at the time of our meeting. He was a bigger individual, much bigger than Judy, and he was prone to occasionally falling and hurting himself. Judy was concerned that she would not always be able to help him get back up on his feet and moving around. Judy had been caring for Bill for quite a while by this point, but she realized that, although she was healthy, she would be unable to maintain the routine. It was just getting to be too much for her.

I see this often, as an elder law attorney. A caregiver becomes worn down and stressed out and starts to deteriorate health-wise even more than the person receiving the care. The caregiver is not only trying to maintain her own life but also care for the person she loves. Something has got to give. So Judy and I began to talk about her situation and how she had been caring for Bill and what her concerns were, moving forward. One of the things that she was concerned about was how she was going to maintain the care. If she could no longer do it, how much would his care cost, and what if she were to run out of money?

She also felt guilty about not being able to take care of Bill alone and trying to bring in outsiders because she and Bill were very private people. She was concerned about putting a burden on her children too. She did not want to ask them to provide care because they had their own kids to care for. Judy did not want her own kids to be burdened with the challenges of the "sandwich generation," the kids who have to care for their parents, their kids, and themselves all at the same time.

As Judy and I were going through our initial discussion, I started outlining the options and the costs of care she might need. She was concerned that if she were to spend this money on Bill, there would be nothing left for her when she needed it. If she were to spend $2,000 or $5,000 or $10,000 a month on Bill's care, at the end of the day, what would she be left with? How would she be able to care for herself? So she was very concerned about whether she would be able to protect her resources against the devastating cost of long-term care.

We went over some of the options available to Judy to pay for long-term-care costs, whether for homecare, assisted living, assisted living with memory care, or nursing home care. Those different levels of care vary in cost. We went over some of the potential payers of long-term-care costs and we also discussed the possibility of Judy's paying for the care herself, out of her own funds. But, unfortunately, after the economy's little bit of a nosedive, she did not have as much in her retirement accounts and her nest egg as she once had. Frankly, if she had had to pay long-term-care costs out of her own funds, she would have been out of money pretty soon.

We also talked about the option of having her kids pay, but she did not want to burden them. We talked about Medicare and how it fit into the equation. Then I asked whether her husband happened to be a veteran and, fortunately, he was. He had served in World War II. He did not go overseas but did serve during wartime. One of the things Judy did not know was that the VA Aid and Attendance benefit could help pay the cost of care for Bill. So, she was delighted to learn of this way to pay for long-term care. She did not have long-term-care insurance, so I told her that Medicare and Medicaid could help pay nursing home costs.

We discussed her legal planning as well. She had an old will and trust that she had created in the 1990s. Frankly, it was pretty out of date in terms of changes to the law. But besides that, it had been drafted from more of an estate planning perspective as opposed to an elder law perspective. The first thing we needed to do was update the financial power of attorney section of the document. We needed to modify it from an elder law perspective.

Judy was also concerned about her house. She had been living in her house with her husband for a number of years and she wanted to make sure that she could protect the house, especially if her husband needed any type of long-term care. She had heard something about Medicaid's ability to take away her house under certain circumstances and she was stressed and concerned about that.

Bill and Judy had three children, including a daughter who lived locally and was a working mother with two young children of her own. Bill and Judy also had two sons, one who lived locally but was not much involved with his parents, and another who lived in California and tried to be involved, but his distance from his parents was a problem. Bill had worked for Ford Motor Company his whole life and had a pension. Judy had been a schoolteacher, and she too had a small pension. They both received Social Security benefits and had saved up a little bit of retirement money, but their retirement account had been hit by the changes in the economy. They had about $400,000 in total assets, plus their two cars and the house they had been living in for more than 30 years. We'll talk more about Bill and Judy a little later on.

CHAPTER TWO

Elder Law versus Estate Planning: What's the Difference?

I started my practice doing strictly high-net-worth estate planning. Many of my clients were business owners and auto executives who were concerned about passing their wealth down to the next generation in the most tax-advantageous way possible, while minimizing hassle and estate taxes.

However, the longer I practiced, the more I was barraged by people asking not "What happens if I die?" but "What happens if I don't die?" I found that my clients all wanted answers to the question of what would happen if they continued to age and face all of the issues that go along with aging, including loss of functionality, long-term-care costs, and living arrangements in care communities.

Elder law, then, is planning for what happens if you do not pass away and continue to age. We take a holistic approach to answering those questions in a process we call life care planning. But the thing to understand is that life care planning is not just about having a lawyer prepare a trust or a will or a power of attorney and then sending you on your way. The approach to developing life care plans at my firm is unique in that I work hand in hand with our elder care coordinator, who is also a social worker.

I take a holistic approach in which we are not just concerned about wills and trusts, or powers of attorney, or Medicaid or VA qualification. That is what typical elder law attorneys are concerned with, but that is all they are concerned with. I handle those things too, but I am also concerned with locating and coordinating care, whether it is in-home care or assisted living care. I am concerned with education. I take the time to educate caregivers on issues such as whether or not Mom or Dad, or some other loved one, should still be driving.

I assist in decision making as well as advocacy to make sure that the loved one who requires care has the best quality of life possible. At my law firm, the focus is more on quality of life than on just moving money or other assets around. My goal is to make sure that your loved one, my client, has the best quality of life possible, and in the case of married couples, that extends beyond the one who requires care all the way to the caregiver. I take our holistic approach to quality of life very seriously, and I give it the respect and attention it deserves in every case.

For example, one of the ways that my firm is unique compared to other elder law firms is the holistic approach we take to planning, which began when a family came to my office to plan for Medicaid help because Mom needed nursing home care. I'm not a social worker. I have social workers on staff now, but at that time, I did not. As soon as the family members mentioned nursing home, I started putting together a plan to qualify Mom for Medicaid and save the family thousands upon thousands of dollars. As our conversation continued, the more we talked, the more I realized that a nursing home was the last place Mom belonged in. She had Alzheimer's, but she was very mobile, though she needed help with daily living activities.

What I did next was pay for a geriatric care manager to go out and perform an assessment of Mom. When the geriatric care manager came back, she said, "Chris, at this point in time a nursing home is not in Mom's best interest. She's incredibly mobile and being confined to a bed is the last place she should be if the goal is to allow her to be happy and comfortable at this stage of her disease. I recommend we try to find her an assisted living community that has a memory care unit."

Well, that one client changed things for me forever. No longer was I going to just blindly put together an elder law plan based entirely on protecting resources without considering quality of life issues. Quality of life would always be the number-one priority for me. In my firm, once we establish a care plan, then and only then will we look at ways to protect resources and secure governmental benefits.

As an elder law attorney, I could have easily put together a Medicaid plan for Mom that would have saved the family thousands of dollars. But would that have improved Mom's quality of life? Personally, I don't think so. One of the maxims that we subscribe to is that individuals want the least restrictive type of care possible. Put yourself in that situation. Would you rather live in the comfort of your own home or a hospital-type environment? Everyone wants the least restrictive type of care possible.

As an elder law attorney, I believe my job is to improve my client's quality of life. My job is not just to get people qualified for Medicaid or any other governmental benefit. In this case, our team improved Mom's quality of life by putting together a plan that placed her in the least restrictive type of care possible. From there, we developed a legal plan to secure government funds in the form of VA Benefits to help pay for the cost of care. VA Benefits brought in an additional $1,000 per month to help cover the assisted living with memory care costs.

This type of planning is very different from the type of planning one would receive from a typical elder law attorney, or estate-planning attorney. Typical estate-planning attorneys would not have a clue where to begin. Typical elder law attorneys probably would have put together a great Medicaid plan and then patted themselves on the back for a great win for the client—even if it meant putting someone in a nursing home who should not be there. How would you feel if you or your mother were in the nursing home? It is important that you work with the appropriate professionals and get advice from the right sources.

I am a Certified Elder Law Attorney, and our firm is a member of the Life Care Planning Law Firm Association. We are in a unique position to holistically meet the needs of our clients, ensuring the best quality of life and best quality of care for people with chronic illnesses. We are uniquely qualified to develop plans for individuals who are suffering from Alzheimer's or Parkinson's or Huntington's disease, or who are concerned about long-term-care costs. We operate from the standpoint of planning, not making decisions only in crisis mode.

A big part of what we do involves documents, so we will frequently use special types of trusts in our elder law planning, whether that means using revocable trusts to plan for avoiding probate (and what happens with your assets if you pass away) or irrevocable trusts, which are more concerned with protecting assets against long-term-care costs. We use irrevocable trusts when we are planning for VA or Medicaid benefits. One of the big goals of elder law or estate planning is avoiding probate.

A lot of people think that estate-planning attorneys and elder law attorneys can draft the same documents because they use similar tools, such as trusts and powers of attorney. Just the other day I was going over a plan for some clients and we were talking about their parents. Dad was a veteran and was suffering from Alzheimer's, and Mom had just broken her hip and had some mobility issues. They were both living in an assisted living community, a continued care retirement community.

Their kids came into my office to talk about protecting some of their parents' resources because they were paying more than $6,000 a month for care. They knew that Dad might need nursing home care in the near future and that the long-term-care bill could easily increase from $6,000 for both of them to $16,000 for both of them.

Their parents had roughly $300,000, and the kids wanted to make sure that if their dad's care level increased and they had to start paying this ridiculous amount of money, Mom would still be able to live in her relatively nice and cushy assisted living community versus the hospital-type environment of a nursing home. They wanted to make sure that Mom still had the quality of life she deserved.

As we developed a plan, we talked about things such as getting qualified for veterans benefits, which could bring in an additional $2,120 a month to help pay for that care. Between Social Security and a pension, they had approximately $4,000 a month coming in, but they were paying more than $6,000 in long-term-care costs.

We put together a plan and I wrote it on my white board for them. I detailed how they could receive an immediate VA qualification that could bring in $2,120 a month. Plus, when Dad entered the nursing home—for skilled nursing—we could put together a plan to qualify him for Medicaid so that Mom would not be impoverished by paying for his care. Instead, his nursing home bill would be picked up by Medicaid.

My clients also wanted to make sure that if both Mom and Dad passed away, their assets would be distributed properly in the way that Mom and Dad had wanted. So, we drafted a plan to reflect those wishes. We talked about the plan and we drew it out on a whiteboard, and I talked about some of the tools that we would use to facilitate the planning.

We talked about a lifetime protection trust, which is a specialized type of trust, and I talked about how we would want to update Mom and Dad's revocable trust just in case, because not all of their assets would go into the lifetime protection trust. Then, I talked about how we needed to update the powers of attorney.

This is where a distinction needs to be made between estate-planning attorneys and elder law attorneys, because the kids had done their own estate planning, and they had come across the common terms of *trust* and *power of attorney*. When we started talking about fees, they wondered whether their current estate-planning attorney could draft these documents. I said, "Maybe, but there is a deep specialized level of knowledge that elder law attorneys and, especially, Certified Elder Law Attorneys have. We need to know more than just how a trust works, or how a power of attorney works. We need to know how that document interacts with different governmental benefits—for example, VA benefits and Medicaid."

As elder law attorneys, we use a lot of specialized types of trusts and we try to simplify the concepts so clients can understand them, but the inner workings can be quite complex. For example, in our practice we use veterans' asset protection trusts, lifetime protection trusts, and Medicaid asset protection trusts. These are all irrevocable trusts that can be quite complex from a tax perspective—from an asset perspective—in terms of setting them up.

A general estate-planning attorney, or your family attorney, probably would not be qualified to assist the family in that situation. It is important to work with a qualified elder law attorney because of the complexities involved. Even though estate-planning attorneys and elder law attorneys use tools that have similar names, there are a lot of differences in how those documents work. I want to cover those documents one by one so you understand the differences.

One of the first documents we deal with is a financial power of attorney. There are lots of different types of financial power of attorney out there. You can download them off LegalZoom for $19.99. However, an estate-planning attorney is not going to spend much time on the concept of financial power of attorney. Estate-planning attorneys think the form is basically a throwaway document. It is going to state that if you get a knock on the head, you will appoint someone, maybe a spouse or maybe your kids, to make decisions for you.

To illustrate the distinction between estate planning and elder law, let's use, as an example, the financial power of attorney. A financial power of attorney, generally, imposes limitations on buying gifts or giving a gift to your family. You are frequently able to gift only $13,000 or $14,000 a year, which is the annual gift tax exclusion amount. As of this writing, that is the amount you can gift without having to fill out a gift tax form.

That version of a financial power of attorney is great if you are young and healthy, and you do not foresee a need to make any gifts. However, if you are a senior trying to qualify for veterans benefits or Medicaid and you want to move your assets into a lifetime protection trust, that transfer of assets is also considered a gift. So, if you are limited to making a gift of only $13,000 or $14,000 for tax purposes and we need to gift $100,000, that financial power of attorney, which may have been drafted by the best estate-planning attorney in your state, is not going to help you meet your goals.

Approximately 9 times out of 10, one of the things we need to do first is to look at how the financial power of attorney was drafted. If there are limitations on gifts, it might be troublesome, when we are in a crisis situation, to figure out ways to bring in different governmental resources to help pay for long-term care.

Another key to reaching our goal is to determine how that financial power of attorney is drafted: whether it is an "immediate" or a "springing" financial power of attorney. Typically, estate-planning attorneys draft springing powers of attorney, which specify that the person you appoint to serve as financial power of attorney cannot act unless two licensed physicians confirm that you are incapacitated. An example of what we often see is Mom naming a daughter as a joint owner on a checking account because Mom still wants to pay the bills, but she also wants to allow her daughter to write checks when necessary.

A potentially better approach, and the way many elder law attorneys would most likely handle it, is through an immediate power of attorney rather than a springing power of attorney, which only becomes effective upon disability and requires having two licensed physicians confirm incapacitation. That way, the daughter would immediately have the ability to write checks for Mom and pay her bills. She would owe Mom that fiduciary duty, and Mom would keep her check-writing ability. The immediate financial power of attorney would not take away Mom's independence or dignity and is often the best route to take.

Financial powers of attorney only cover incapacity. A trust can cover not only incapacity but also the management and distribution of assets after the loved one has passed away.

There are a lot of differences in the way that trusts are drafted. Let me give you some examples. Generally, this is what we see. A typical estate planning revocable trust might be set up to take care of generation-skipping taxes or estate taxes, and to avoid probate, which leaves everything outright to the surviving spouse and, after that, maybe to the kids. Well, that is great, but what happens if that surviving spouse is in a nursing home? Everything in the trust goes outright to the nursing home, not the surviving spouse. At the very least, the surviving spouse is not able to use that money.

Often, a well-qualified Certified Elder Law Attorney will create a revocable trust but will also build in a special type of trust called a *safe harbor trust*. What that safe harbor trust will do is protect the surviving spouse if the surviving spouse is receiving long-term care and is in a nursing home. In that scenario, the surviving spouse would not receive the money outright. Instead, the money would be held in a special type of trust whereby the surviving spouse could receive Medicaid benefits but would also have a pot of resources in the safe harbor trust to pay for additional services or improve his or her quality of life. The other option is leaving the money outright to the surviving spouse, who then would have to pay it directly to the nursing home.

As elder law attorneys, we look at and handle deeds very differently from the way estate-planning attorneys do. Your typical estate-planning attorney might just draft a deed directly into a revocable trust. He might say, "Okay, great, I avoided probate," and call it a day. As elder law attorneys, we are also concerned with the ramifications and the future of the estate recovery and of trying to qualify our clients for different governmental benefits.

We frequently use specialized types of deeds, such as a legacy deed, which is a deed designed to avoid probate and estate recovery and go to the revocable trust or the beneficiary upon the death of, say, Mom or Dad. We also might put that deed, that house, that property, directly into a lifetime protection trust so that we can protect it from any type of nursing home spend-down, or spend-down to qualify for veterans benefits.

Estate-planning attorneys and elder law attorneys might use similar types of documents, but the way they operate, the way they prepare those documents, is going to be very different. If you are caring for a loved one with a chronic illness—perhaps that person has just been diagnosed with Alzheimer's or dementia—it is important to understand that legal documents must be drafted from an elder law or elder care perspective versus an estate planning perspective.

You do not want the services of an attorney who helps business owners pass down their businesses and who focuses on planning for estates worth $5 million if your loved one has only $300,000 and has been diagnosed with Alzheimer's. Your loved one is going to have completely different goals from those of the business owner. It is very important to understand the distinction between an estate-planning attorney and an elder law attorney.

Probate is a court administrative process that deals with assets that do not pass through joint ownership, a beneficiary designation, or a trust. Typically, probate can take five months to a year to settle. It can be costly. The national average for costs that get eaten up in a probate case is 3 to 5 percent of all assets. Those costs can be court costs, inventory fees, attorney fees, and publication costs, among others. So yes, probate can be pretty costly. Also, probate is a public process. A lot of people value their privacy, but probate is a court process in which anyone can gain access to those public records.

A lot of people do not understand just how easy it is for something to end up in probate. One of the services that elder law attorneys offer is ensuring that nothing ends up going through the probate process. For example, family members could inherit property or buy a new condo up north—something as simple as that—and fail to inform the attorney. The next thing they know is that they're in probate.

There are four arrangements for transferring assets out of the name of someone who has passed away. The first is a joint ownership. The second is a beneficiary designation. The third is a trust. If the asset does not pass through one these, it ends up going into probate, which, as we discussed, is a court process that involves inventory fees, court costs, and attorney fees.

It is amazing how time-consuming probate can be and how things can just drag on, especially when real estate is involved. This is not to say that those involved are not doing a good job, but when a large family is involved, there can be disagreements.

For example, if Mom has a house that is in her name only when she passes away, and it ends up going into probate, what happens if one of Mom's three children wants to sell the house and the other siblings do not want to sell the house? What happens if they want to hold off because they think the market is going to improve?

I have probate files sitting on my desk that have been in probate for years just because the family has not decided to sell the house. Every year we have to go to court and request continuances, and the family members have to pay the attorney fees to do so. They have to pay the court costs too. It can be a pain—and a pain in the pocketbook. If everything had been set up properly and handled, most likely, through a revocable or irrevocable trust, the whole probate process could have been avoided.

We also have what is called living probate. Probate not only can affect you when you pass away, but also when you become incapacitated. If, say, you get a knock on the head and you cannot make any financial or medical decisions and you have not appointed someone to make those decisions for you through a financial or medical power of attorney, the only alternative would be for someone to go to court and get a guardian or conservator appointed to manage your financial and medical needs.

That is another court process that will become public record, and you will have to pay associated attorney fees and court costs. Also, a judge will oversee the actions of your guardian—usually a loved one. We avoid that living probate situation through proper disability documents: the financial power of attorney and the medical power of attorney.

Another concern many people have with estate planning, or elder law, is taxes. They want to minimize the amount of taxes they have to pay, whether that means an inheritance tax, an estate tax or income tax. As long as you have less than the maximum estate tax exemption amount, you do not have to pay the so-called death tax. As of this writing, the maximum estate tax exemption amount was $5 million for an individual. Typically, on the elder law side of planning, most people do not have more than $5 million, so it is less of a concern for elder law or elder care planning than it is for estate planning.

This is not to say that we do not deal with tax issues when we are dealing with elder law issues. In fact, we deal with a lot of tax issues, including income tax issues related to retirement accounts. A lot of our clients have IRAs and 401(k)s and pretax dollars. In doing our elder care planning, sometimes we have to look at liquidating those accounts or moving them around and paying the taxes all at once or over a number of years.

It is important to understand that you have a mortgage, basically, on any type of retirement account, meaning that you have not paid taxes on those funds. You have to pay the income tax at some point. Sometimes, it is beneficial, as part of the planning for the senior—or Mom or Dad—to pay the income tax now rather than deferring payment or arranging to have the kids pay the income tax in the future. Income tax is a big issue in elder law.

Also, we talk about gift tax quite a bit in elder law, because money frequently moves around. It moves between the generations, from individuals to trusts. Generally, gift taxes have an annual exclusion amount. In 2013 that amount was $14,000, meaning you can give $14,000 to as many different people as you like with zero gift tax due. You do not have to fill out a gift tax form. If you are married, that tax-free amount becomes $28,000, which you can gift to as many people as you desire.

If you gift more than that annual gift tax exclusion amount, you probably still will not owe any gift taxes because, in addition to your annual gift tax exclusion amount, you have a lifetime gift tax exclusion amount, meaning you can give a certain amount of money away over your lifetime without paying any gift tax. Currently, that lifetime gift tax exclusion amount is $5 million. Most of my elder law clients—in fact, all of my elder law clients—have much less than $5 million.

Even if you give more than the annual gift tax exclusion amount, all you would need to do is fill out a gift tax form to say that the recipient of your gift used a portion of his lifetime gift tax exclusion amount and, therefore, will owe zero gift tax.

We talk about gift taxes when we are dealing with elder law, but, in reality, gift taxes have little consequence. Much of the planning we do is gift tax neutral, meaning we are not going to pay any gift taxes. However, we do have to deal with income tax, as I discussed.

Also, we need to understand the differences between an individual income tax rate and a trust tax rate. If assets or income are generated inside a trust, and the proceeds are held inside that trust, the trust pays income tax at a compressed tax rate. This means that the trust is going to reach the maximum tax percentage at a much lower amount.

Much of the planning that we do in elder law involves the use of special irrevocable trusts, which normally would be associated with trust income taxes. But a good elder law attorney will make sure that the planning is set up to replace trust income tax rates with individual income tax rates. We do this through specialized uses of trusts and some complexities built into those trusts.

Elder law attorneys do not necessarily need to be familiar with things such as generation-skipping taxes or estate taxes—taxes that estate-planning attorneys are familiar with. We do, however, need to be familiar with income tax, retirement accounts, gift taxes, and trust income tax issues.

Another concern of elder care planning, or estate planning, is pets. Sometimes loved ones happen to be pets rather than children. With proper planning we can make sure that the senior's furry friend—a horse, a dog, a cat, or a turtle—can be cared for by the person, or persons, specifically chosen to take custody. This is, usually, the best way to go where pets are concerned, especially because it avoids the possibility of euthanasia. Sometimes we can even put together an animal care trust so that money is set aside for a pet's care by a chosen caretaker after the owner has passed.

Actually, when I started my practice, one of my first clients was a wonderful woman in her mid-60s. She had a fair amount of life insurance. She was not married at the time, but she had four children, and she felt that all four of them were derelicts. She was the first one to admit that they were kind of a mess. They had drug issues, faced back child support, were in and out of jail, were convicted of drunk driving, arrested all the time, and could not hold down jobs.

She had more than a million dollars, and she did not want to leave the money outright to these kids because she knew they would just blow it. She was a cat lover and loved her two cats dearly. She knew that in her extended family, among her siblings and others, there were 26 cats. I still remember that number today, about eight years later.

She set up her trust so that a portion of it would go to the Humane Society and a portion of it would pay for health insurance for all 26 cats in her extended family. Pet health insurance would be paid for out of this million and a half dollars, and then she set aside a quarter of a million dollars for the care of her cats. Yeah, lucky cats.

As for her kids, she wanted to give them one last chance. She had four children and each child had a chance to inherit a quarter of what was left over after that the cats were taken care of, which was about $200,000.

The kids would have to jump through all of these hoops within a year to receive that $200,000: If the trustee determined it necessary, they would 1) have to go through rehab, 2) pay all of the back child support, 3) secure gainful employment, 4) stay out of jail, and 5) actually do community service at the Humane Society or a similar type of nonprofit organization for the benefit of animals. If they did not jump through all of these hoops within a year, their portion of the trust would also go to the Humane Society. That interesting woman is still alive.

That case was pretty extreme, but I have created more trusts for cats than any other animal. Pet trusts frequently revolve around cats. I have not created any for dogs. My firm has set up trusts for many horses, because a lot of upkeep and expense goes with owning a horse. My partner has set up trusts for a lot of dogs and horses. We have had some birds, but most often the trusts center on animals that have a longer life expectancy, such as horses, or just are really a part of the family, such as cats and dogs. And every once in a while, of course, a turtle is involved.

Recently, I thought of another animal trust scenario. We have not done one of these at the firm, but someone in my family bought one of those turtles that live for approximately 200 years. If that is not a reason to have some type of trust set up, then I do not know what is. Those turtles can easily outlive their owners. How will those turtles be cared for when their owners are gone?

How do people know which route is best for them? All those who are concerned with long-term-care costs should incorporate some sort of elder care planning into their own planning. For example, discussing long-term-care insurance is something people should do while healthy and able to afford it and qualify for it.

Likewise, planning involves important discussions regarding the types of trusts that will be used. The big difference in deciding whether to go with straight estate planning or more of an elder care or elder law approach depends on whether you are concerned about long-term-care costs now or anticipate them in the future. In either case, you would need to incorporate long-term-care planning into your overall plan.

The earlier you start planning for your retirement years—before you are in crisis mode—the more options you have, whether you are planning for Medicaid or for VA benefits. Generally more options mean a better-quality plan, a better-quality life.

A family was referred to my firm by a financial planner who knew the type of work that we do and, particularly, that we focus on improving seniors' quality of life, especially if they have been diagnosed with a chronic illness. The financial planner referred a husband and wife to us. The wife was still working and her husband had been diagnosed with early Alzheimer's. He still had the ability to function quite well. If you were to have a conversation with him, you would not be able to tell that he had been diagnosed with this disease, but the signs were there. His ability to function would become progressively more limited and he would need more care. There was no question about it.

This couple came to us pretty much as soon as they received that diagnosis. We were able to put together a plan, using a specialized type of trust—a lifetime protection trust—to ensure that the money they had worked so hard for over their lifetime would be protected and used as efficiently as possible. They had thought they would be all set for retirement, but they had not taken into account the possibility of a nursing home bill of $10,000 to $13,000 per month if the husband's Alzheimer's continued to progress.

What we were able to do was set up a lifetime protection trust with the idea that the husband had a number of years before he would need that level of care. You can think of it almost like a piggy bank. We moved their assets into a piggy bank.

We could then confidently tell that family that even if the husband's condition worsened and he needed long-term care, they were not going to be completely impoverished. With that type of plan in place, we would, theoretically, be able to protect everything that was put into that trust if the husband could avoid skilled nursing care for five years. Based on the way his condition was progressing, we felt fairly confident that he could make it through those five years.

The family had peace of mind, knowing that at least a portion of those resources, the portion we put into that piggy bank, would be protected. They knew that although they would march down the long-term-care road one day, the costs would not impoverish them.

Now let's compare that to many of the families who come in to us in a crisis situation, in which they have already been spending, unnecessarily and for a number of years, maybe $10,000 a month on care. If they had visited us earlier, when they first received the diagnosis of Alzheimer's, we could have protected more of their resources. Generally, the earlier we start planning, the more options we are going to have.

In another case, Mom was left with only about $80,000 worth of assets and had already sold her home and made gifts to some of the grandchildren for their college education. The family came on behalf of Mom, because Mom was in a nursing home. They said, "Chris, we're running out of money. We don't really know what to do. We're paying $10,000 a month and we're almost out of money."

Luckily, they came to me because the social worker at the nursing home had suggested they see an elder law attorney. The Medicaid program looks back five years to see if any gifts were made. In this case, as grandmothers do, Mom had made financial gifts to her grandchildren for their college education, not to try to qualify for any type of governmental benefit. Unfortunately, that kind of gift creates a divestment penalty, meaning that because she made those gifts, even when she runs out of money, Mom cannot qualify for Medicaid immediately. Most families do not realize this.

Who pays that penalty? Will the grandkids give back the money that they already used on their college education? Probably not. Will the kids be left holding the bag? Luckily, because the kids came to see me before they ran out of money, we were able to put together a plan, not to protect any of their resources but to save the grandkids from having to give back the money. The kids, also, would not have to kick in the money to erase the mistakes they did not even know they were making just because they had not visited an elder law attorney earlier.

A lot of the rules with regard to Medicaid, the VA, and different governmental benefits are completely illogical and draconian. A grandmother will want to give money to her kids or grandkids for their college education or their church, or to help them buy a first house. But the way the rules work, if she does this, regardless of whether she is trying to plan for Medicaid, she will be penalized.

Sometimes the work we do is not protecting resources but cleaning up messes. If families would come in earlier and approach the elder care continuum from a planning perspective versus a reactionary or a crisis perspective, we would have better options, and we would be able to save more money. Unfortunately, the system is kind of broken in the sense that the more money you have, the more options you have, and the more options you have, the better your quality of life will be.

Compare getting diagnosed with Alzheimer's or Parkinson's or some other type of chronic illness to having a heart attack. We have insurance programs that will pick up the majority, if not all, of the expenses of a $100,000 surgery bill after a heart attack. If you are diagnosed with a chronic illness such as Alzheimer's, you might have long-term-care insurance, but that is not really the answer. We do not really have a good system for handling the expenses of chronic illness and long-term care.

This is where a Certified Elder Law Attorney comes in. We can help create an even playing field when these rules do not make any sense. The earlier you come in and discuss these rules with us, the earlier you will understand how the programs work. We can help you avoid the pitfalls of this elder care journey. We can also do some proactive planning to try to insulate you against long-term-care costs and the mistakes that we see people make.

In sum, the earlier you plan ahead, the better the chance that your loved one who needs care will have the best quality of life possible. Failure to plan is planning to fail. Too many families operate from a crisis mode when it comes to long-term care, and many families have found that if they had come into my office two to three years earlier, I could have protected more of their resources for their loved one and even brought in additional funds to help pay for long-term care.

The Elder Care Continuum

What we do as an elder law firm and a life care planning firm is help clients with what is called the elder care continuum or the elder care journey. Many of our clients are going through a similar journey, depending on what type of chronic illness or aging issues they are dealing with.

Our clients often are suffering from some type of debilitating disease—whether it is Alzheimer's, Parkinson's or Huntington's, or multiple sclerosis—that has started to limit their ability to function. Many times, they will not recover from it or even improve. Rather, their functionality will decline and they will have different types of care needs, which will, naturally, lead to different types of long-term-care costs. One of the things I do as a Certified Elder Law Attorney and a life care planning attorney is help people understand what their future may hold as it relates to the type of illness they face.

The commonest chronic illness that many of my clients suffer from is Alzheimer's disease. Alzheimer's disease affects the mind and can steal memory, change personality, and be quite debilitating for many of our clients. There is no cure for Alzheimer's and people who have been stricken by it become more debilitated as time goes on.

From an elder law perspective, there are certain procedures we need to follow for clients with Alzheimer's, including updating powers of attorney and making sure their documents are drafted from an elder law perspective rather than an estate planning perspective. The ability to sign any type of legal document requires legal mental capacity. Alzheimer's is a progressive brain disease that destroys memory, thinking skills and, eventually, the ability to carry out even the simplest tasks, including the ability to feed oneself.

Alzheimer's disease is a form of dementia, which is a broader term used for a variety of debilitating cognitive diseases. Dementia comprises a whole slew of symptoms caused by disorders that affect the brain. It is important to understand that dementia is not a specific disease, but a group of symptoms. Loved ones suffering from dementia may lose their problem-solving ability, be unable to dress or eat without help and unable to think well enough to perform normal activities. Alzheimer's disease is a fatal brain disease that affects more than five million Americans and is the most common form of dementia with no cure.

At the earliest stage of Alzheimer's disease, your loved one may experience problems relating to memory, thinking, or concentration. The disease destroys brain cells, which can cause problems with memory, thinking, and behavior that, in turn, can affect life, work, relationships, and decision making. When their loved one is first diagnosed, Alzheimer's families often face tremendous issues with respect to financial security, as well as the emotional fallout from the diagnosis. Generally, what I have found is the earlier the diagnosis, the more emotional the fallout a family has to endure.

So, in Bill and Judy's case, Bill was suffering from Alzheimer's and that is why Judy wanted to come into my office and sit down and talk. She understood that the diagnosis of Alzheimer's disease can be a difficult elder care journey to go through, considering the long-term-care costs and difficult decisions that need to be made. When your spouse's personality and memory change, he or she can seem almost like a completely different person. Judy was dealing with the stress of not only that but also of how she would care for Bill at home and for how long, and how she would pay his medical bills. She wanted to make sure that Bill had the best quality of life possible.

So, when she came into our office, we sat down and talked about the disease and how it was affecting Bill, as well as the potential long-term-care costs that she would be facing. She was very stressed and concerned about those long-term-care costs. One of my roles as an elder law attorney is to address those concerns and develop a plan to offer peace of mind. I wanted to convince Judy that even though her husband was diagnosed with Alzheimer's and facing all of the issues that go along with it, there was hope. There was light at the end of the tunnel, and it was not necessarily a death sentence for a certain quality of life that she expected. So through proper legal planning we can protect quality of life for the person who is suffering from Alzheimer's as well as the person who is providing care for the Alzheimer's patient.

Another chronic disease that we help many of our clients with, from a legal perspective, is Parkinson's disease, a neurodegenerative disease that is similar to Alzheimer's in that it involves long-term-care concerns. It can cause gradually increasing loss of functionality. From a legal perspective, the planning for someone suffering from Parkinson's disease is very similar to the planning for an Alzheimer's patient. In both cases, we need to make sure that we have proper documents in place so that if our client loses legal mental capacity, we have the ability to make legal decisions on his or her behalf and are also able to take the legal steps necessary.

Parkinson's disease is another form of brain disorder that occurs when certain nerve cells in the brain become impaired, often affecting dopamine production. When 80 percent of one's dopamine-producing cells are damaged, the symptoms of Parkinson's disease start to appear. Typically, the symptoms of Parkinson's include tremors, slowness of movement, rigidity, balance issues, shuffling, stiff facial expressions, and depression.

Similar to Alzheimer's or dementia, when a loved one is diagnosed with Parkinson's, there can be denial, anger and depression, not only in the loved one who needs care, but also among the patient's family members who must deal with the change in circumstances. It is important to understand that the loved ones have little control over the disease, and neither do the caregivers. Being clear on this can prevent future frustration. The sooner acceptance of the new lifestyle occurs, the sooner the family can start part planning accordingly.

Parkinson's disease really hits home for me, personally, because I had a family member who was affected by it. He was a business owner who also owned a lot of real estate. He was a successful businessman, but as he started to age, he began to suffer the symptoms of Parkinson's. Right around the time his condition began to worsen, the downturn in the economy happened. Basically, his real estate investments went under just when he needed additional services and Parkinson's was really taking effect.

The changes in the economy and his growing long-term-care costs really put additional strains and stresses on the family. If he had taken proper precautions prior to meeting his long-term-care costs, we would have been better able to protect his resources, and he would have had a better quality of life as he took the elder care journey and dealt with his Parkinson's disease.

Multiple sclerosis (MS) is yet another chronic condition that affects many of our clients. MS is an autoimmune disease that can affect the brain and the spinal cord. It affects people differently, depending on its location and severity, but, like Alzheimer's and Parkinson's, it is a debilitating disease that can cause the loss of functionality. Because of that simple fact, we must take legal steps as proactively as possible to ensure that we have the flexibility to plan and protect our clients' best interests, keep their quality of life as high as possible, and, at the same time, offer as much peace of mind through planning as we possibly can.

MS is one of the more unpredictable chronic diseases in that its attack on the central nervous system can lead to numbness in the limbs, paralysis, and loss of vision. Often, multiple sclerosis follows a series of stages. The first stage is, frequently, relapsing-remitting MS, characterized by clearly defined attacks of worsening neurologic function. Following that stage is primary progressive MS, characterized by slowly worsening neurologic function. Next comes secondary progressive MS, characterized by steady worsening, leading to the stage of progressive relapsing MS, in which the disease is in its final stages with clear attacks and worsening neurological function.

There are many concerns when caring for a loved one who is aging or dealing with a chronic illness. There are many chronic illnesses that can affect a loved one, but the net result is that all create a need for proper legal planning.

Continuum of Care

Chronic illnesses and general aging demand many different levels of care. That care could start at home with some additional help from a spouse, a family member (such as a son or a daughter), or a neighbor, or even from someone just popping in occasionally to check on the chronically ill senior.

Informal daily care is often provided first by a family member or friend. You may be this caregiver. You may be helping a loved one with the activities of daily living. A 2006 AARP study reported that between 30 and 38 million adult caregivers currently provide informal care. On average, caregivers provide 21 hours of care per week, and more than 1,000 hours per year. The study reported the estimated economic value of the care to be about $350 billion.

If you are a caregiver, you need to think not only of the amount of time you are spending on the care but also of some of the other components of caregiving. For example, the AARP study found that about half of nonspousal caregivers reported spending about $200 per month of their own money on groceries, medicines, and other necessities for the care recipient.

On top of the sometimes hidden, out-of-pocket expenses a caregiver needs to consider are his or her lost wages when it is necessary to scale back at work in order to maintain the caregiving schedule. Scaling back your time on the job can lead to loss of job security, wages, career advancement, employment benefits, and retirement income. Still later, the effects can manifest themselves in the loss of value of 401(k) plans, IRAs, and pensions, ruining the chance for you to have a normal retirement.

Even worse than the financial effects of caregiving are the health effects. Often, I've discovered in my practice, caregiving causes the caregiver's health to suffer. Caregivers generally begin to suffer their own health effects and many times report problems with depression. Is this you?

As a person's condition deteriorates, he or she might start to need increased levels of care. Let's say a person starts off living at home and is relatively healthy, but then some home help is required. To reiterate, that help could come from a family caregiver, but often families look to commercial homecare companies to bring in additional services. Home care companies might provide a couple of hours of care a day, a couple of times a week, or even around-the-clock care. The cost of that service would depend on the amount of care being provided. Typically, home care costs $18 to $25 per hour. That might sound expensive, but most people prefer to live in the comfort of their own home. As an elder law attorney, my job is to improve quality of life for all parties involved and, generally, that means keeping the loved one who needs care in his or her home, where your loved one is more familiar with the surroundings. This alone can aid in quality of life. Plus, generally, home health care is less expensive than institutional care.

If the senior's health condition worsens and he or she needs an increased level of care, sometimes a transition to an assisted living community, or an independent living community with home care provided, make sense. Assisted living communities vary in terms of quality and the level of care they provide. Often, they provide a protective environment where the senior's meals can be taken care of, and medication can be administered. Some assistance with daily living activities could include bathing and showering and getting dressed, as well as taking care of incontinence issues. The cost of an assisted living community varies, depending on the level of service provided, but, generally, the cost runs anywhere from $1,500 to $5,000 per month per individual.

If a senior is suffering from any type of memory issue, transition to an assisted living community that provides memory care makes sense. Here, the key is the protective environment. Almost the entire population of such living communities consists of people living with memory issues caused by Alzheimer's or dementia. Such a facility can provide a whole host of services, but the protective environment is most important. The cost of an assisted living community with memory care could be anywhere from $5,000 a month to $7,000 a month per individual.

So, independent living and assisted living involve a whole continuum of levels of care and costs associated with those levels. The two types of community—independent and assisted living— vary a great deal. More and more we see independent living communities offering home-care types of service a la carte, which blurs the lines between independent living and assisted living communities.

So you might pay one fee to the facility for rent and meals and the protective environment, and then a separate fee to an independently contracted home care company that comes in and provides additional services, such as bathing, incontinence management, and medication management. This new hybrid form of living can present challenges when trying to qualify for things such as veterans' benefits. But it is a way that seniors can age in one location, where they start off living relatively independently, but as they need additional services, they would not have to transition to another community. They could receive those services a la carte from a home care company.

Another option is a continued care retirement community, which provides not only independent living, but also assisted living and nursing home care, all on one property. So the lines between the different types of living communities are beginning to blur and each community can be a little bit different. And that is where working with an elder law attorney who practices from a holistic standpoint will help you make sense of the different communities and figure out which community best fits your situation in your area.

The final stop, in terms of housing based on medical necessity, is a nursing home, which is also called a 24/7 skilled care facility. There, the atmosphere is closer to that of a hospital than that of an assisted living community. In a nursing home the rooms contain hospital beds, and more skilled nursing care is available. The cost of this type of facility can range from $7,000 to $10,000 a month per individual.

There is a big difference between assisted living facilities and nursing homes. Assisted living facilities look more like hotels, with some of them even featuring chandeliers and big staircases. They offer more of a home-type environment than a nursing home, often with comfortable furniture, attractive artwork, and plenty of activities. In a nursing home, comfort is less of a concern, as safety and medical necessity take precedence. Nursing homes are more clinical looking and offer 24-hour skilled nursing care. That service trumps all others in a nursing home.

Nursing home communities also offer rehabilitation, so that when patients suffer an acute illness that sends them to a hospital for three days, they can get on the road to recovery through physical therapy. That three-day hospital visit is important to note because the third day triggers the Medicaid benefit. When a qualified Medicaid recipient spends three days in a hospital, Medicaid pays for his subsequent rehab in a nursing home. This is important because nursing homes can cost $7,000 to $10,000 a month per individual.

One of the roles of an elder care firm is trying to link up the level of care that individuals need with their level of function, in addition to helping them understand the costs. All of these different communities have different costs, and within those communities, different levels of care have different costs. For example, for home care the cost could range from $1,000 to $3,000 a month. This would be for home care for a couple of days a week, a couple of hours a day. Compare that to an assisted living community, where the costs might rise as high as $5,000 a month. An assisted living community with memory care might jump to $7,000 a month, and a nursing home could cost as much as $10,000 a month. I don't care how much money you have. If you are paying that type of fee every month, it is going to eat at your nest egg pretty darn quickly.

Thankfully, we have a few ways we can pay for these levels of care. Of course, anyone is welcome to enter a private pay situation, in which all bills are paid out of pocket. But as I just mentioned, that is a sure-fire way to crack your nest egg in a hurry. On top of that, as we know, with the changes in the economy, not everyone has as much money as in the past. So private pay will not be a viable option for many people.

The second scenario would be for the senior's children to pay. Some parents have wealthy children who are willing to provide for Mom or Dad's care. But that is also a rare situation. It is not that the children would not want to help their parents; they often just do not have the money to do so, especially if they have a family of their own.

Next, we have long-term-care insurance. Unfortunately, not as many people have long-term-care insurance as probably should have it. It has been expensive in the past and, these days, it is difficult to qualify for. For people who have no other means to pay, there is Medicare. But Medicare is not a long-term-care provider. Medicare pays for short-term rehabilitation only.

Military veterans and their spouses can take advantage of the VA benefit, which can pay up to just over $2,000 a month for long-term care. Finally, there is also Medicaid, which can pay for skilled care in a 24/7 nursing home. That is the only type of facility that Medicaid will cover the costs of, actually, so it is limited, as many of the other options are.

In Bill and Judy's situation, Bill and Judy are both on the continuum of care, and our first step is to identify where each of them is in terms of functionality and health. When they came into our office, Judy was relatively healthy. In other words, she did not need any care. She was fully independent, but Bill was starting to march down the continuum to more limited functionality. He needed someone around him at all times to prevent him from harming himself. He was not able to prepare his own meals anymore. He was starting to be forgetful and was becoming a wandering risk.

He was farther along the first line of the continuum, which measures the level of functionality, or health. He needed additional care from the start. Judy was getting worn down from being the full-time caregiver, so we needed to look at going to the next step, which would involve bringing in additional help around the house for as long as possible. In Bill's case, this took the form of having one of his daughters provide private-duty home care. She came in to relieve Judy.

So the daughter began to provide home care, and at this point, because Bill was a veteran, one of the opportunities available to us was to qualify Bill and Judy for the VA benefit. That benefit could bring in an additional $2,054 a month to pay the daughter for her time, because she was taking time out of her life and away from her work. We put together a personal care contract stipulating that the daughter be paid for her time, but those costs would be covered by the VA benefit.

As Bill's condition worsened and 24/7 care at the house was no longer medically feasible for Bill's safety, we had to transition him to an assisted living community that provided memory care. He needed to be in a more protective environment that would provide the best care and the best quality of life possible. With this change came additional costs, but, at least, Bill was in a better position and receiving a better level of care. This also freed up Judy from some of her caregiving duties so that she too could have a better quality of life.

The Necessary Legal Documents for Those Suffering from Chronic Illness

There are some key legal tools and legal documents for those concerned about long-term-care costs, those suffering from chronic illnesses, and those who are just getting older and suffering from limited functionality.

This may be a review, but the takeaway from reading this book is knowing the key legal documents your loved one needs to plan for the long-term-care legal journey he or she is facing.

The first tool is a financial power of attorney, which appoints someone to make financial decisions on another person's behalf. There are two types: springing financial power of attorney, and immediate financial power of attorney.

A springing power of attorney is a financial power of attorney that springs into being only upon a certain condition, which, typically, occurs when two licensed physicians attest to the fact that the person who created the financial power of attorney is incapacitated. Upon the physicians' confirmation of incapacitation, the successor or agent-in-fact—the person appointed to make decisions for the senior—then has legal authority to sign checks, work with the attorney, buy or sell real estate, and, basically, manage and control anything that is included in the financial power of attorney document.

Let's compare that to an immediate financial power of attorney, which becomes a power of attorney the moment it is signed. The individual who signed it has given power to the person appointed as agent-in-fact to act on the individual's behalf. In this case, no physicians are required to confirm incapacitation because an immediate power of attorney does not require incapacity. The springing financial power of attorney always requires incapacity; the immediate power of attorney never does.

It is also important to understand that not all financial powers of attorney are created equally. For example, in our elder care firm, one of the first things we do is review the financial power of attorney that has been put in place by the family. Probably, 9 times out of 10, we find that financial power of attorney is severely lacking because it was created from an estate planning perspective as opposed to an elder law perspective.

Again, estate planning is planning for what happens if you were to pass away, and elder law is planning for what happens if you do not. A financial power of attorney drafted from an estate planning perspective may talk about gifts of up to the federal gift tax exclusion amount or it may discuss the planning for estate taxes and it may limit gifts that the attorney can grant to himself, or it may discuss Medicaid planning or VA planning. A financial power of attorney that was created from an elder law perspective is going to list what an attorney can do in terms of planning for Medicaid or veterans benefits, or for long-term-care costs.

This is not to say that attorneys who draft the financial power of attorney from an estate planning perspective are planning incorrectly. It is just that they do not understand all of the considerations that go into elder law. A financial power of attorney could be drafted by the best estate-planning attorney in the state, but if he or she is not cognizant of the most pertinent elder law issues, they won't be included in that financial power of attorney.

It is very important that the financial power of attorney is well drafted and very specific in its listing of powers because you will want this document to be effective. If you want to use a financial power of attorney document at a bank, it is important that you have the powers specifically listed because the bank is going to be in a "cover our butt" mode—very cautious. The bank is going to be concerned about someone other than the account owner making changes or writing checks. It is important that the financial power of attorney be specific in its power.

It is worth noting that when individuals sign a financial power of attorney, they are not giving up any rights. What they are doing is giving rights or powers to someone they have appointed as a financial power of attorney. In the case of a springing power of attorney, again, the document is not legally effective until incapacitation has been determined by two licensed physicians.

Drawing up an immediate power of attorney does not forfeit an individual's rights. As the creator of a financial power of attorney, you will still be able to write checks and buy and sell real estate as you normally do. With the immediate power of attorney you have allowed someone else to do that on your behalf. And you can also do it on your own behalf. But the person you have appointed to serve as a financial power of attorney has a fiduciary duty to act on your behalf. This means that person cannot go out and buy himself or herself a convertible with your money. The money must be used for the benefit of you, the person who created the financial power of attorney.

In the financial power of attorney document, you can grant, basically, any power or ability that you yourself already have. That is why it is important to be very specific when you grant powers so that you understand what abilities you are giving your agent-in-fact. Often, one of the important powers to list is the ability to make gifts. To whom can the person with financial power of attorney make gifts? Can that person make gifts to himself or herself or to family members?

Also, it is important to know whether the financial power of attorney document you signed allows changes to your estate planning. Can the person you have appointed as financial power of attorney create a trust on your behalf? Can he or she create a will on your behalf? Whether he or she should be able to or not will depend on your situation. That is something that often differentiates a financial power of attorney document drafted from an estate planning perspective from one that is drafted from an elder law perspective.

If you sign a financial power of attorney document, you can always change your mind, assuming you still have the mental capacity. The person you appointed 5 or 10 years ago, or the person your loved one has appointed as power of attorney, assuming that appointed person is still mentally capable, can execute a new financial power of attorney to appoint someone else to serve as agent-in-fact, or decision maker.

The next tools in elder law planning are medical directives. These are the documents that appoint someone to make medical decisions for you if you become incapacitated, as well as decisions about end of life. We have what is called a medical power of attorney, which is similar to the financial power of attorney in that you appoint someone to make decisions on your behalf. However, this document comes into play only if you become incapacitated. Also, we want to create a living will, or use living-will language to indicate your end-of-life wishes. Here, the question is whether you want life support to keep you alive. Would you wish to remain on life support or not?

The famous Florida case of Terry Schiavo was a legal struggle involving prolonged life support that lasted from 1990 to 2005. It happened because Terry Schiavo had no legal documentation indicating her end-of-life wishes. She had no medical power of attorney, or living will, or any document containing living-will language.

In February 1990 Terry collapsed and suffered massive brain damage due to lack of oxygen. She was in a coma for two-and-a-half months. For the next couple of years doctors tried to rehabilitate her through therapy, but the treatments failed to change her vegetative state. The reason the case dragged on for so long and attracted so much media and public attention was that her husband wanted to remove her from life support, specifically, a feeding tube, while her family did not. Her family wanted her to remain on a feeding tube.

Prior to this, Terry's husband had a wonderful relationship with her parents, who even allowed him to stay in their condo, rent free, for several months. After many years of rehab efforts that failed to make any impact on Terry's condition, her husband, in June 1998, petitioned the court to remove her from life support, citing the fact that she remained in a vegetative state.

However, the family fought him, requesting that she remain on life support. This became a court battle that lasted for years. In the initial court battle, Terry's husband won the petition and actually had his wife removed from life support. The court case was resolved. However, the family appealed that ruling and the feeding tube was reinserted. After numerous petitions and even some changes to the law, Terry's feeding tube was only finally removed in 2005, when her family ran out of appeals and other legal avenues to fight the court's decision. On March 31, 2005, Terry Schiavo finally passed away.

In this case, a five-year or seven-year court battle could have been avoided had Terry Schiavo spent some time setting up a legal advanced medical directive, or other document, using living-will language. All she would have had to have done was visit an estate-planning attorney for probably a half hour to an hour to prepare what is called a medical power of attorney, or living will, which generally can be prepared in a day or two for less than $500. Instead, her heartbreaking ordeal turned into a legal proceeding that dragged on for a number of years and became a big court battle in which the only winners were the attorneys who were receiving fees all those years.

Another important document to have is called a HIPAA authorization. HIPAA stands for Health Insurance Portability and Accountability Act, which came into the picture around 2004. Since then, when you become a new patient at a doctor's office, you are required to sign a privacy waiver. What happens if you do not sign that privacy waiver or do not give that HIPAA authorization? Well, the medical facility will not be able to share your medical information with the people you have named in your medical directives. So you need HIPAA authorization in addition to a medical directive and financial power of attorney. These are what we call disability documents, and anyone over the age of 18 needs them in place in case they are ever unable to make medical decisions for themselves.

As we age, this kind of issue pops up more and more, so these documents are especially important for seniors and should obviously be taken care of prior to loss of ability to function. If you do not have these legal documents in place, the alternative recourse is a court proceeding for conservatorship, in which someone would have to go to court and open up a guardianship with regard to medical decisions. If we have these documents in place—the financial power of attorney, medical power of attorney, living will and HIPAA authorization—we can avoid having to go to court on a lot of these issues, which will save the family time, money, and stress.

In addition to planning for incapacity, we need to also plan for passing away. That is where wills and trusts come into play. The documents previously discussed are what we call disability documents. They plan for what happens if you become incapacitated. The next set of documents plan for what would happen if you were to pass away. The first of these documents is a will or a last will and testament. When someone passes away, there are four ways in which assets can be transferred out of their name: through joint ownership, a beneficiary designation, a trust, or probate. What I did not mention, you may have noticed, is a will. A lot of people think a will avoids probate. Well, it does not. A will is what gives instructions to the probate court on how to administer your estate.

If you have only a will-based estate plan, it is important to understand that someone may have to take a trip to the probate court, which will oversee the processing of your will. It can be costly and time consuming, and it is a public process, in which anyone can get access to the deceased's court records. Typically, a probate will take anywhere from five months to a year to run its course.

On average, 3 to 5 percent of any assets going through probate can get eaten up in court costs, attorney fees and publication costs, among others. Also, anyone can gain access to court documents to see which assets are going through probate. If you have only a will or a will-based estate plan, that, typically, is going to be your ticket to probate court. To reiterate, a will does not avoid probate.

It gives instructions to the probate court on how to administer your estate.

As I mentioned, the probate process generally takes five months to a year, and the probate process starts when someone goes to court to be appointed as a personal representative. If a will is involved, it must be recorded along with the death certificate and it includes language identifying the personal representative. Filing fees are associated with this process. When no will exists, the deceased dies intestate, meaning "without a will." Each state has a default rule designed to figure out who among the willing candidates should be appointed as a personal representative.

Once that personal representative is appointed, he or she is now in charge of gathering all of the assets in order to inventory them for the probate estate. This can be a difficult and time-consuming process, and that is why we recommend to many of our clients that they start to get their parents' and their own financial affairs and assets organized so that when a loved one passes away it is not a matter of going through a shoebox to figure out what assets that individual has. Once the personal representative has wrapped his or her arms around all of the assets that are in the deceased's name, they then have to prepare an inventory that is submitted to the probate court.

Also, around this time, a notice needs to be sent out to let creditors know that a probate estate has been opened. This goes out to all of the known creditors, and, typically, is published in the local newspaper. This is yet another reason that probate should be avoided—because it requires you to notify all known creditors.

When the personal representative files that inventory, he or she must pay an inventory fee to the probate court. The fee is a percentage based on the value of the assets going through probate. One probate estate I handled involved just one account, but we had to write a $1,500 check to the county probate court. That fee could have been avoided through a trust-based estate plan.

After the inventory has been filed and no objections have been raised, a statutory amount of time needs to pass before the personal representative is allowed to distribute any assets. In Michigan you need to wait four months after the notice to creditors has been filed, and five months before you can actually distribute any of the assets. Assuming everything goes well—all of the creditors have been paid off, proper inventory has been taken, all the fees have been paid—then and only then can you start distributing the assets and close the probate. And, typically, it takes somewhere between five months to a year for that probate process to run. Contrast that to a trust-based estate plan, which can, theoretically, be opened and closed within a couple of weeks.

This is why many people want to set up a trust-based estate plan or a living trust. A good way to think of a revocable living trust is to think of it as a suitcase. You can put your assets into this suitcase, hold on to it while you are alive, and make changes to it at any time. But if you were to pass away, you pass that suitcase on to someone else, a person called a trustee, to administer those things as per your desires, as per the instructions indicated in your trust document.

One of the big advantages of setting up a trust is that 1) you can avoid probate, and 2) you can have a lot of control over the distribution of the assets. For example, instead of just leaving everything outright to your beneficiaries, with a trust-based estate plan, you can do some neat things in terms of protecting your beneficiaries against lawsuits, creditor action and loss of assets due to divorces. You can also protect the beneficiaries against their own poor financial mismanagement of the assets by appointing someone else as the trustee.

Some of the major tools we elder law attorneys use are special types of trust. Typically, we use what is called an irrevocable trust, which differs from a revocable living trust. There are additional benefits available in irrevocable trusts, but like most things, there are also some trade-offs, some sacrifices, for those benefits.

You can use what is called a lifetime protection trust if you are trying to protect resources against long-term-care costs and you are relatively healthy. The advantages of the lifetime protection trust are that you can obtain qualification for veterans' benefits almost immediately. At the same time, you can start what we call a five-year clock. If you can make it five years without setting foot in a 24/7 skilled nursing facility, all of the assets that are held in that lifetime protection trust will avoid nursing home spend-down or Medicaid spend-down.

The Medicaid spend-down or nursing home spend-down is a process whereby a senior has excess assets and spends all of his or her money on nursing home care to qualify for Medicaid. Then, once on Medicaid, he or she can keep $2,000 in assets and $60 per month in income. In other words, once you qualify for Medicaid, you can pay for a haircut each month—not much. There are better options than the dreaded Medicaid spend-down—for example, a lifetime protection trust, in which the assets would be protected. The lifetime protection trust basically acts like a piggy bank in which we can protect assets against future long-term-care costs. While the trust is an irrevocable trust, meaning you cannot make changes to it, you can break open the "piggy bank" and get access to those assets at any time. It is a trade-off. There is a loss of control in the sense that you cannot make changes to the trust once it is set up, but you still have the flexibility to unwind the trust and get the assets out when you need them. By unwinding the trust, I mean that all of the assets can be taken out of the trust and given back to the person who needs care. You also could create a new lifetime protection trust with different terms if need be.

Our tools also include a Medicaid asset protection trust, and a veterans' asset protection trust—both specialized types of trusts that we use to help qualify clients for VA or Medicaid benefits. Again, they are irrevocable trusts. But they are typically used in crisis situations, in which long-term-care is already being paid for.

In Bill and Judy's case, if we had set up a lifetime protection trust two, three, four, or five years earlier—if they had come to see me five years earlier than they actually did—all of their assets would have been protected. They would have been protected from any type of nursing home costs and I could have gotten them qualified for VA benefits immediately.

I cannot say it enough. One of the most important points to take away from this book is that the earlier you visit an elder law attorney, the more planning options you have. Many times, those planning options involve the use of specialized types of trusts. It is good to have options—time and options.

As we go through this elder care journey, one of the things we often do is plan for what happens if a loved one passes away. More often than not, we look at a trust-based estate plan to efficiently manage the estate administration in order to get the assets out of the loved one's name when that person passes away. That way, we avoid having the probate court control the distribution, and thus we allow the estate to go to the beneficiaries in the way the deceased loved one wanted it to go while also minimizing any taxes.

Once you understand this elder care journey, you need to understand the six ways in which we can pay for long-term care. The first option, which we discuss in Chapter 5, involves using your family money to pay for long-term care—sometimes the children help pay for care for a loved one.

Private Pay and Children's Funds

T he cost of long-term care can be devastating to families and it will only increase over the years. One way to cover it is to pay out of your own pocket, which is called private pay. Although a lot of people have tried to save during their working years and may have built up big retirement funds, the downturn in the economy and the fact that people do not save as much as they hope to save makes private pay not an option for many. If you have the money and you are wealthy, then private pay certainly is an option. But there are other options too.

Sometimes children are willing to help pay the cost of their parents' care, but more often than not, parents do not want to be a burden to their children or put this financial burden on them. Something to keep in mind is that elder law attorneys consider the ways clients can pay for long-term care. What happens when one spouse is sick and the other spouse is healthy?

For example, in the case of Bill and Judy, Judy is 10 years younger and has a long life expectancy, while Bill is facing long-term-care costs. If Bill has to pay $10,000 a month, and they have $300,000 dollars total, what is Judy going to do after private-paying for a number of months, or even years, for Bill's care? This is why private paying—just paying out of your own funds—might not always be sufficient to cover the entire cost of long-term care. As an elder law attorney, I look at ways to preserve my clients' nest eggs, using every resource that we have available.

A number of years have passed, maybe six years, and Bill still receives care at home. He transitions into assisted living with memory care when living at home is no longer the best option for him.

The VA benefit continues paying $2,054 a month. It helps Judy continue to maintain a certain quality of life while still covering the cost of Bill's care. When Bill's health declines further, he needs 24/7 skilled care, and this is when he enters a local nursing home.

Now, the great thing is that when he enters the nursing home, because of the planning we did earlier, he is able to immediately qualify for Medicaid even though Judy possesses nearly all of their resources, which are way over the asset limit. Through planning and the special type of asset protection trust we put in place six years ago, Bill and Judy qualify immediately and do not have to pay the $10,000-a-month nursing home bill that normally would be due, and would drain Judy's assets.

At the end of the day, Judy has peace of mind from knowing that even though Bill's long-term-care costs are extraordinarily high, she will be protected from having to pay them. She can enjoy peace of mind, knowing that she can continue to enjoy good quality of life, even as Bill receives the appropriate care that he needs.

Of course, not everyone plans ahead as Bill and Judy have. In that same situation, if a husband were to enter a nursing home without doing any type of planning, the family could be on the hook for $10,000 or $11,000 a month in nursing home costs.

Options are available, however, when someone enters a nursing home without having created a financial plan. Let's look at the example of Matt and Rose.

Matt is suffering from Parkinson's. While Rose is still relatively healthy, Matt enters a nursing home and Rose comes into our office because she has been referred by a social worker at the nursing home. She is concerned about long-term-care costs. Matt and Rose have $200,000 worth of countable resources. Rose is concerned that if she is paying $10,000 a month for Matt's care, she will not have anything to live on, moving forward. They have not done any type of planning other than creating powers of attorney and a will.

Rose's options include paying $10,000 a month until she is basically impoverished (not a good option), or putting together a Medicaid plan whereby nearly 100 percent of her assets would be protected from long-term-care costs.

This is what we did, using a specialized type of trust called a sole benefit trust, which stipulates that as long as Rose is healthy and living in the community while Matt receives care in a 24/7 skilled nursing home, we can funnel the assets to Rose so she will not be impoverished.

The only thing she will lose is the patient pay amount, which is Matt's payment to the nursing home every month. It comes from his Social Security benefits and pension, which, in this case, is only $2,000. Matt and Rose will pay $2,000 a month to the nursing home versus the $10,000 a month they would have had to pay had we not set up a sole benefit trust. It gives Rose the peace of mind to know that, moving forward, she will be able to maintain her quality of life.

That is what we can do for a married couple. It is different for a widow or single individual. Let's look at Julie's case. Julie is in a nursing home suffering from multiple sclerosis. She has been there for six months and her son and daughter are concerned about the high cost of care and that they are running out of assets. Julie has $150,000 worth of assets and a house, and they want to obtain additional services for her, but they do not want the money to run out. Assets of $150,000 may seem like plenty to pay for long-term care. However, if you're paying $12,000 per month in long-term-care costs, you need to understand that when the money runs out, so do the options.

In Julie's case, we can protect some of the resources. We use a specialized type of legal plan that enables us to protect roughly half of the assets. The plan allows half of the assets to be used for the costs associated with a single individual in a nursing home and the remainder of the assets to be protected and used to pay for additional services if necessary. Also, if the nursing home patient were to pass away, those assets could be passed down to the next generation.

We can protect Julie's liquid assets, and we can protect her house from estate recovery. If the state pays any costs of care, say through Medicaid, the state can place a lien on a house. The lien has to be paid off before the next generation can do anything, including selling the house. By using a specialized type of deed called a legacy deed, we can maintain that exemption from Medicaid during Julie's lifetime and also avoid the estate recovery when she passes away.

The net effect is that we can protect more than half of the liquid assets, as well as the family home, versus the alternative in which Julie would have just paid the nursing home every month until she was left with only $2,000. The state would come in after she passed away to take away the home. Julie's family members are very happy that they sat down with a Certified Elder Law Attorney to review their options.

Even if you do not plan ahead and are operating from a crisis standpoint, there are still options available. But planning ahead is always—always—the best course of action.

The private pay option for long-term-care planning is straightforward: patients must cover their health-care costs out of their own assets. Generally, people hold assets in different locations. They may have a 401(k) or an IRA, which we call qualified funds or retirement accounts. Both of those accounts can be sort of tricky when planning for elder care, because they generally deal with pretax dollars, meaning income tax has not yet been paid on them.

Many times, when we put together an elder care plan, we have to move money around. If we are moving pretax dollars, we have to pay the income tax before we move the money. Families may also have nonqualified money, which could be mutual funds, stocks, bonds, or other investments that they have already paid income tax on. Generally, from the standpoint of elder care planning, this type of asset is easier to maneuver and protect.

A missed opportunity for many families is not realizing that life insurance often has a cash value. Life insurance carries a death benefit, obviously, and when you pass away, the policy pays a sum of money. You can sometimes cash in that policy before it pays out. Many people do not realize this.

When we are trying to qualify for a governmental program such as Medicaid or veterans' benefits, it is important to figure out exactly what the cash value is. Families often come into our office to talk about the different assets they have and they fail to mention the cash value they have in life insurance. It is very important to understand this concept, and it is something we bring to the attention of our clients, often to their surprise.

Most families have checking and savings accounts as well as primary residences. Sometimes people also have an additional piece of property, a vacation home. When we put together an elder care plan, it is important to document all of these different assets, because the different governmental benefits have different requirements in terms of which assets are exempt or which assets are supposed to be spent down.

Typically, your primary residence is an exempt asset, but if you were to own a second home, that house would have to be sold to pay for long-term care unless a strong legal plan has been put together ahead of time.

It is the elder law attorneys' job to help clients understand just what they have in terms of assets, because these assets can be spread out among different accounts and different forms of ownership. Our goal is to simplify the planning and streamline everything so that we have a firm understanding of which assets are in that client's name. That allows us to properly plan and protect those resources.

In addition to assets, people can use their income to pay for long-term-care costs. Generally, we see two types of income. We see income from Social Security benefits, which can be claimed at retirement age, and we also see pension income, which, of course, becomes active upon retirement.

These are two income streams that we cannot do much legal planning around. In the case of pensions, you can name your spouse and take a reduced benefit. You also can take early retirement, which could affect your Social Security benefit over your lifetime. But other than that, there are not many options where Social Security and pensions are concerned.

Some people like to include the minimum required distributions from IRAs or 401(k)s as income, but in reality, those assets are not true income. When planning for elder care, it is important to understand the distinction between what an asset is and what income is, because Medicaid and veterans' benefits have particular rules for each type of asset and income.

Wouldn't it be great if we all had enough money to self-fund the catastrophic cost of long-term care? Unfortunately, with the ever-increasing cost of long-term care, private paying or relying on our children to pay for long-term care may not be feasible. However, there are other ways to pay for long-term care that we'll cover in this book.

CHAPTER SIX

Long-Term-Care Insurance

Long-term-care insurance is a great tool for paying for long-term care. It is a product created specifically for the cost of long-term care. It is a piece of the puzzle but not the entire answer. I am a great believer in long-term-care insurance. I have long-term-care insurance myself, even though I do not foresee myself setting foot in a nursing home tomorrow or anytime soon.

One of the reasons that I obtained this insurance so early in life was to make sure I locked out any preexisting conditions, which is one of the first issues with long-term-care insurance. With the changes in the long-term-care insurance industry, fewer people are able to qualify for it due to preexisting conditions, which could include diabetes, osteoporosis, or even taking antidepressants. Each insurance provider has its own requirements for preexisting conditions that would disqualify an individual or hike up his insurance premium. The key to understanding long-term-care insurance is exploring it before needing it because of the restrictions regarding preexisting conditions.

The second problem with relying only on long-term-care insurance is the cost. Long-term-care insurance can be rather expensive, depending on the underwriting, the type of insurance that you are buying, and your age. Also, the costs have been increasing. You might start paying at one rate, but your premium could increase. For example, in my office, my partner's parents had long-term-care insurance, and everything was fine. But then they received a 40 percent rate increase followed by an 80 percent rate increase the following year.

If you are a senior on a fixed income and have a budget in place, you may not be prepared for those increases, especially at a time when you may need the insurance the most. You are going to be in a tough spot when you have to decide whether you want to continue to pay for that long-term-care insurance or save your money.

Another issue with long-term-care insurance is that the policies are very different and not many people understand exactly what their policy covers. For example, a long-term-care insurance policy could pay, maybe, only $50 a day, and a nursing home could run to $220 a day. There may be caps on the daily rate, and there also may be a monthly, annual, or lifetime cap on what that long-term-care insurance will pay out.

Also, there may be elimination periods during which long-term-care costs must be paid for 30, 60 or 90 days before the long-term-care insurance triggers. The events that trigger long-term-care insurance vary—from requiring someone to provide help with up to two daily living activities to helping with incontinence issues, or feeding or showering. Only when those things are taken care of will the long-term-care insurance trigger. Long-term-care insurance payouts also vary. A policy may be set up on a straight reimbursement basis, whereby you pay the bill and the long-term-care insurance company reimburses you. In other cases, a company may just pay you cash directly, once you have triggered the long-term-care insurance policy.

Typically, the sweet spot for purchasing long-term-care insurance is somewhere between the ages of 40 and 65 because more reasonable prices are available for people in that age group. Again, to qualify for long-term-care insurance, applicants will to have to satisfy some underwriting requirements and prove that they have no preexisting conditions that may disqualify them.

Long-term-care insurance is definitely a tool and a piece of the puzzle, but it is not the magic-wand answer. However, if you can qualify for it, long-term-care insurance is definitely something that you should look into. I was 33 years old when I got long-term-care insurance. I do not know anyone who got long-term-care insurance at that age. I am pretty far ahead of the curve. But if you are a business owner, you can get some tax deductions for long-term-care insurance, which is nice.

With all of the changes going on in the long-term-care industry, there are some new products available, some hybrid products that combine long-term-care insurance with life insurance policies. One of those products is Lincoln Money Guard, which has some nice advantages. In the past, a common concern of people planning for elder care was that long-term-care insurance was a "use it or lose it" proposition. People who ended up not needing any payouts from their long-term-care insurance providers came to the cruel realization that they had paid that money—those years of premiums—for no reason. And they would never see that money again.

The new hybrid policies reduce the long-term-care insurance benefit but, at the same time, add a death benefit. This means that whether you pass away or cash in the policy before you die, you still will receive about the same amount. So either way, theoretically, you can get your money back.

One of the problems with these policies is that they are new and largely untested. This is how long-term-care insurance was in the past—new and largely untested. And we have seen how the long-term-care insurance industry has basically blown up with skyrocketing premiums and companies folding because they did not fully understand the product when it was put together. They were making actuarial guesses and did not realize that so many people would be needing long-term-care insurance benefits. And so, the long-term-care insurance industry has been rocked.

There is a similar uncertainty about the hybrid policy's feasibility in the long run. And there is nothing worse than paying for a financial product that is no longer viable when you need it. There are hybrid policies out there that sound great, but there are many things that should be considered before purchasing one.

Also, it is important to understand that hybrid policies do not provide true long-term-care insurance. If you are looking for a pure, long-term-care insurance benefit, your money might be better spent on a traditional long-term-care insurance policy. Another option would be to get a long-term-care insurance policy plus a separate life insurance policy.

Laurie came to my firm with the intention of planning for her mom, who needed home care. Laurie was gathering all of the assets and trying to wrap her arms around what her mom had. She found out that her mom had a long-term-care insurance policy, and she was very excited about that. She thought everything would be okay. But when we actually reviewed the policy, we found that Laurie did not understand what her mom had, nor did her mom understand what she had.

Laurie's mom had a policy with an elimination period of 180 days. What that means is that Laurie's mom had to pay out long-term-care costs for 180 days before the long-term-care insurance policy kicked in. And once it did kick in, it was only going to pay out $50 per day for up to $100,000. Already, Laurie was paying about $80 a day for her mom's home care. So the long-term-care insurance policy was not going to be a short-term answer because Laurie and her mom would have to wait half a year before being able to receive the insurance benefits. And then, even when the benefits were triggered, they were not going to cover the entire cost of the long-term care.

Luckily, Laurie's mom, Eunice, was the widow of a veteran, and because of that, we were able to qualify her for the surviving spouse benefits. So, she was able to receive $1,000 a month from the VA. This would help supplement that gap between her long-term-care insurance and her long-term-care costs. So, the veterans' benefit works wonderfully with long-term-care insurance and proves, once again, that there is no single, true answer. It is always just a matter of putting these puzzle pieces together to come up with the best plan.

A husband and wife came to my firm because they were concerned about long-term-care costs for their mom, and we put together a great plan for them to bring in veterans' benefits. Caregivers, whether they are sons or daughters, are usually in their 40s or 50s, or sometimes, their 60s. One of the things I always bring up to them is that now is the time they should start looking into long-term-care insurance for themselves, because they are in that sweet spot where the premiums make a lot of sense. On top of that, they are at that age when most people can qualify. As preexisting conditions continue to eliminate people from qualifying for insurance policies, it is important to look at these things as early as possible.

When that couple came in to talk about Mom, I recommended that they look into long-term-care insurance for themselves. Both of them seemed completely healthy to me and did not have any health issues that I was aware of. So, I thought they would be perfect candidates to explore long-term-care insurance.

I referred them to a long-term-care insurance expert, and surprising news came back. The wife was not able to qualify because she had taken an antidepressant medication. Neither of them had ever had cancer or any other major diseases or surgeries. But because of that one medication she was taking, or had taken in the past, she did not qualify for long-term-care insurance. Even I found this very surprising. A lot of people, including myself, are not aware of all the circumstances that can disqualify their applications for certain long-term-care insurance policies.

The lesson here is that it is important to explore long-term-care insurance while you are healthy and as young as possible.

Medicare

A lot of people come into my office thinking that Medicare is the answer to their long-term-care costs. There are several different types of Medicare, including Medicare Part A, Medicare Part B, and Medicare Advantage Plans. However, here we are talking about a very specific form of Medicare, and that is the Medicare that pays for nursing home stays.

To qualify to receive nursing home benefits or rehab from Medicare, you need to meet certain requirements. The first requirement is you have to have been admitted to a hospital for more than three days. It is important to be actually admitted and not just there under observation, because we have seen this latter scenario cause problems. *Observation* is not going to trigger Medicare. The patient needs to be *admitted* to the hospital for three days.

This three-day rule can be very tricky for families who are unaware of it, because, often, a hospital will keep patients for observation only and not admit them. It is important that the family or caregiver fight to make sure the patient is actually admitted if there is a chance the loved one will need rehab or a nursing home stay after he or she is discharged from the hospital. If you do not reach that trigger for Medicare, that three-day stay, you could be paying $250 a day for rehab, completely out of your pocket. After a three-day hospital stay, Medicare will pick up the first 20 days at no cost, and then, possibly, require a co-pay from you for days 21 to 100.

After a patient is admitted to the hospital, whether for a broken hip or some other ailment, he or she can qualify for Medicare and receive rehabilitation in a 24/7 skilled nursing facility. Medicare pays up to 20 days of rehab in a nursing home, assuming continuous progress is made. If a patient fails to improve, Medicare can end payments sooner, but, generally, assuming that the patient participates in the rehabilitation, he or she receives up to 20 days of rehab in a nursing home, covered by Medicare.

For a nursing home stay between 21 and 100 days, patients can receive Medicare benefits, but a co-pay would be required, unless supplemental insurance picks up the cost of the co-pay. That co-pay would be roughly $150 per day, which is a pretty hefty cost. But if patients have supplemental insurance to cover the cost of the co-pay, they can receive up to 100 days of Medicare-paid rehab in a nursing home at absolutely zero out-of-pocket costs. However, after 100 days, Medicare would come to an end and this is what a lot of people do not realize. Medicare is a short-term payer of nursing home costs but is not the answer to any type of long-term-care costs. This benefit of Medicare falls under Medicare Part A.

A good example is the case of my client Fred and his family. Fred's family came into my office because Fred had gone back into the hospital after falling and fracturing his collarbone. The family was concerned that because of Fred's age, 90, and his dementia, he might not be coming back out of the nursing home after going into the hospital. He was admitted to the hospital for three days and he was going to transition to a nursing home for rehab. The family wanted me to explain the process to them again, to help them understand how Medicaid and Medicare would work to pay for Fred's long-term-care costs.

I explained that Medicare generally pays up to 100 days' worth of short-term rehab in a nursing home, after the patient has been admitted to a hospital for at least three days. In this case, Fred met that requirement. But Fred had also fallen less than 60 days before, for which he had also been admitted to the hospital for three days and discharged to a nursing home for rehab. Unfortunately, after his second fall and rehab, Fred was not able to tap into his Medicare for any additional support because Medicare requires that a patient stop receiving Medicare benefits for a certain amount of time before starting a second short-term rehab of 100 days.

In this case we had to immediately put together a plan to try to qualify Fred for Medicaid so that he would not have to pay the full $10,000-a-month nursing home bill. We also wanted to protect some of his resources to pay for additional services over and above what Medicaid would pay.

CHAPTER EIGHT

Veterans' Benefits

M any of our clients are seniors who served during a period of war, whether it was World War II, Korea, Vietnam, or the Persian Gulf conflict. There are two little-known benefits to veterans and their surviving spouses if the veterans meet certain requirements: the Veterans Aid and Attendance benefit, and the Pension for Non-Service-Connected Disability for Veterans.

Not many elder law attorneys talk about veterans' benefits with their clients. Certainly, many estate-planning attorneys have no idea about these little-known benefits that are available to veterans and surviving spouses who face long-term-care costs.

Attorneys were first allowed to begin counseling veterans and surviving spouses in 2008, as accredited VA attorneys. I was one of the first attorneys in my state to be a VA-accredited attorney. It is important that the attorney you work with is VA accredited and therefore allowed by the US Department of Veterans Affairs to counsel veterans.

There are a lot of non-attorneys out there who talk about being a "veterans specialist" or "VA specialist." They help prospective clients complete their VA application at no charge, but, often, what they are doing is helping with the application and then persuading families to buy high-commission insurance products. Most often, these products make no financial sense for the veteran or the surviving spouse or the family. Their sole purpose is to provide a large commission for the insurance salesman. The products often have no relevance for the family or their future Medicaid planning.

Often, these non-attorneys make a mess of clients' finances by selling high-commission annuities with long surrender periods that tie up assets. It is very important to know the source of your information on veterans' benefits. Unfortunately, just going down to the VA administrative offices might not necessarily help you understand how to secure these benefits, because, quite often, the administrators put roadblocks between you and your benefit. This is where a Certified Elder Law Attorney can help.

There are two primary types of veterans' benefits that pay money on a monthly basis. One is the service-connected-disability benefit and the other is the nonservice-connected-disability benefit. Service-connected-disability benefits are available to veterans who received some type of injury while in service, or were disabled later, after, say, they were exposed to Agent Orange while in service. They are almost like workman's comp for the military.

If you were to be hit by a bullet during your military service and lose the use of a shoulder or a limb, you would receive compensation for that and a disability rating, which would determine the amount of compensation you would receive each month. It could be anywhere from a very low amount, practically nothing, to a couple of hundred dollars, to more than $3,000 a month.

That is not really the benefit that I, as an elder law attorney, deal with. What I deal with more is the Pension for Non-Service-Connected Disability for Veterans. This benefit is available to veterans who meet certain requirements. First of all, the veteran needs to have served 90 days of active duty. One of those days needs to have been during a period of war. Finally, the veteran cannot have been dishonorably discharged.

A lot of people have questions about the requirement of "one day during a period of war." Congress has established dates of service that qualify and they are available on the congressional website, but, basically, if individuals served one day during World War II, one day during Vietnam, or one day during Korea, they qualify. They would not have had to serve outside the United States. As long as they served in the military during one of those periods of war, they would satisfy the "one day during a period of war" requirement. They also would have to have served on active duty. In other words, they could not have been in the reserves. They must have served on active duty for at least 90 days, not necessarily consecutively. And again, they could not have been dishonorably discharged. Those are the easy requirements for the veteran.

On top of that, the veteran, or the surviving spouse of the veteran, must pass an income test. The VA looks at the amount of income the veteran has coming in every month, and that needs to be offset by the amount of ongoing long-term-care costs or unreimbursed medical expenses that the veteran or the surviving spouse is paying out each month. There is a formula for figuring out the maximum allowable pension rate for a veteran or surviving spouse. Once that figure is determined, income must be subtracted, and that new figure will be the veteran's benefit amount each month.

A single veteran could be entitled to a little more than $1,700 per month, tax-free. A married veteran could receive more than $2,000 per month, tax-free. The surviving spouse of a veteran could receive more than $1,100 per month, tax-free. These numbers change yearly and go up with inflation in the same way Social Security does.

There is an additional asset test in which the VA looks at the number of countable resources the veteran has. If they are over a certain amount, the veteran will not qualify. Typically, a single veteran, or a surviving spouse, can have between $30,000 and $40,000 in countable assets. A married veteran can have somewhere between $60,000 and $80,000 in countable resources. Countable resources for VA purposes include, basically, everything except the value of a home, automobile and personal possessions.

To qualify as the surviving spouse of a veteran, the surviving spouse needs to be a widow or widower. The spouse cannot be divorced from the veteran. If the veteran passed away and the surviving spouse remarried, the spouse would not be able to claim veterans' benefits. If the surviving spouse were to remarry a veteran, the surviving spouse might be able to claim on the second marriage.

The VA programs are a great way to pay for home care. If a family is paying somewhere between $1,000 and $3,000 a month to a commercial home care company, the VA is a great resource to turn to. A VA benefit can even be used for family caregivers in cases in which Mom or Dad is the veteran or surviving spouse and one of the kids is providing care. One of the strategies we can employ is setting up a care contract so that children are paid for the care they provide and the VA reimburses the veteran for that cost of care.

We also do a lot of VA benefit planning when a veteran, or surviving spouse, is in an assisted living community and might be paying somewhere between $2,000 and $5,000, or $5,000 to $7,000 if the assisted living care includes memory care. The maximum VA benefit depends on whether the payee is a single veteran, surviving spouse of a veteran, or a married veteran. The VA benefit is great for people who are paying for home care, which might max out at $3,000 per month, but the VA benefit is just a drop in the bucket if 24/7 skilled care in a nursing home is involved.

One of the great things about the VA benefit is that there is, currently, no look-back period. A veteran could be "over" in assets today, but we could put together a legal plan and life care plan that includes a special asset protection trust. Then the veteran could be "under" in assets and qualify, based on the resource test the following month.

As I previously mentioned but will provide more detail here, when Bill and Judy initially came into my office, Judy was the sole caregiver for Bill, but one of their daughters, who was living nearby, eventually began providing additional help. Judy needed some relief, and was not always able to take care of Bill. Because

Bill was a veteran who had served 90 days of active duty, one day during a period of war, and was not dishonorably discharged, there was a chance that Bill would qualify for the VA benefit.

However, there were two stumbling blocks in Bill's way when he and Judy first came to my office. The first was that they were not paying any long-term-care costs. Even though their daughter was providing care, no money was exchanging hands. The second issue was that their assets were over the VA's countable assets limit.

However, I talked to them and learned more about the services their daughter was providing. Even though she was not a nurse, she was basically providing private-duty home care. That is a level of care that can help trigger the non-service-connected disability benefit.

To help Bill and Judy qualify for the benefit of $2,054 a month, we put together a plan that included a care contract in which Bill and Judy agreed to pay their daughter for her services. She was taking time off work and working fewer hours, sacrificing her own money to provide care for her parents, which many of our caregivers do.

However, we needed to put into writing a personal care contract that would qualify them on the income test for VA benefits, because, now, Bill and Judy were paying more money per month to their daughter than they had coming in from Social Security and Bill's pension. That qualified them on the income test for the VA benefit.

The last stumbling block was the asset test for the veterans' benefit. To pass the asset test, a married couple must have less than $80,000 worth of countable resources, and Bill and Judy had more than that. However, we put together a lifetime protection trust, otherwise known as a VA asset protection trust. We positioned their assets properly inside that trust and, after getting the trust funded, Bill and Judy could qualify based on the asset test as well.

The great thing about that plan was that we were not only planning for the veterans' benefit, but also for future Medicaid benefits. Medicaid has a five-year look-back period, during which any gifts can be viewed as a divestment. With that in mind, setting up a care contract can be complex because money exchanges hands between parents and family members. It's important that this exchange is not viewed as a divestment. If we have a properly drafted care contract that meets all of the requirements, money can change hands without being a divestment; it is payment for a service.

Also, there may be a potential Medicaid issue when we transfer money into a special trust. The trust needs to be set up so that it will not be harmful to a future Medicaid application. Many times, when seniors start out on an elder care journey, they bring in home care. From there they may transition to assisted living, but, often, the last stop is the nursing home. They need flexibility so that if they were to qualify for the veterans' benefit today, they would still have the flexibility to eventually qualify for Medicaid when they entered a nursing home. They need to be able to enjoy this benefit without having to worry about divestment penalties.

Because Bill and Judy came to my office as soon as Bill was diagnosed with Alzheimer's, and as their family was starting to provide additional services, we were able to qualify them so that they could receive an additional $2,120 a month, tax-free, to help pay for that cost of care. Not only did I get them qualified for that VA Benefit, but the planning that was done also helped protect their assets from the long-term-care costs of a nursing home and Medicaid spend-down.

Medicaid

While the VA benefit is great for paying for home care or assisted living, it is lacking when it comes to paying for the entire cost of 24/7 skilled nursing care—generally the last stop on the elder care continuum. If the loved one enters a 24/7 nursing home, we generally look to a different governmental program to help cover the cost of that care. That program is Medicaid.

Often, people confuse Medicaid and Medicare. Medicare is a program that helps pay for short-term rehabilitation in a nursing home, while Medicaid is a long-term-care program that helps pay nursing home costs if a loved one remains in a nursing home and does not return home.

Medicare pays for short stays in which patients might spend a month or two in a nursing home, receiving physical therapy and rehabilitation. Their objective is to be discharged to return home or to an assisted living community.

As mentioned previously, Medicaid is difficult to qualify for and the application process can be draconian with its very difficult rules concerning asset limits and look-back periods and certain requirements. Many families find the rules befuddling, especially the IRS's rules regarding gifts.

For example, for a single person to qualify for Medicaid, he or she is allowed to have only $2,000 worth of countable resources. Married couples with one spouse receiving nursing home care and the other spouse living, healthy, in the community are allowed to have more than $2,000 worth of countable assets, depending on their situation. Generally, they are not allowed to have more than just over $100,000 worth of countable resources. If they have more than that, they have to cut their assets in half before qualifying for Medicaid.

The question is what is a countable resource or a countable asset? For Medicaid purposes, it is very similar to the VA definition: everything is a countable resource except for the primary residence, automobile, and personal possessions. You are also allowed a small amount of the cash value of your life insurance and you are allowed a prepaid funeral as long as it is through an irrevocable funeral contract. Everything else is a countable resource for Medicaid purposes, including most of the cash value of life insurance, which a lot of people do not realize.

A person's house does not count toward that $2,000 asset limit, but all the states now have what is called a state recovery. This means that while the home may be an exempt asset while the owner is alive, when that person, the Medicaid applicant, passes away, if the state has paid any of the costs of care, the state can now place a lien on the house and be reimbursed for whatever it paid out.

If Mom spends five months on Medicaid in a nursing home with the state paying $10,000 toward her cost of care, when Mom passes away, the state can put a lien on her house for $50,000. So, proactive steps need to be taken to try to preserve the house after Mom or Dad passes away.

Medicaid is difficult to qualify for, and it is not a program in which you can be "over" in assets today and then give away all of your assets and be qualified for it tomorrow. There is a 60-month, or five-year, look-back period to see if any gifts have been made. If a gift has been made, even if it was not made for the purpose of qualifying for Medicaid, it remains a countable asset. For example, let's say Grandma gives little Johnny $20,000 to help pay for college. For Medicaid purposes, that is a gift, even though Grandma may not have been planning to go into a nursing home or planning for Medicaid benefits.

Medicaid looks at the amount that has been gifted over the five years prior to the application for benefits and assesses what is called a divestment penalty, in which Medicaid takes the amount gifted and divides it by the average cost of nursing home care in the applicant's state. In Michigan this equates to roughly $7,500 per month.

If you have given away $75,000 over the previous five years, for any reason, you divide that sum by the divestment divisor amount of $7,500. This comes to 10, which represents the number of months the applicant needs to wait before qualifying for Medicaid nursing home benefits—meaning the applicant will have less than $2,000 worth of countable resources. The state will not pay any cost of care until that divestment penalty runs the course of those 10 months. After those 10 months, the state will cover the cost of care. The idea here is that if Mom or Dad gifted money to the kids, the kids are going to have to give the money back or pay for the nursing home care.

Medicaid does not pay the entire cost of care. Medicaid looks at the amount of income that an individual has coming in and then attributes it to what is called the patient pay amount, which is the amount that needs to be paid to the nursing home. However, Medicaid will leave applicants with $60 a month of their own income. If you have a Social Security income of $1,500, Medicaid is going to take all of that $1,500, apply it to the nursing home cost and then pick up the rest. But Medicaid applicants are allowed to keep $60 a month of their own income, which pays only for a haircut, basically. This is where Medicaid planning comes into play. It allows us to protect some resources and have resources available to improve the quality of life for the person receiving care.

Medicaid application documents can be picked up at the Department of Human Services or online, but there is more to the application process than just the application itself because applicants often have to answer to caseworkers and explain some of their prior transactions. Caseworkers can look back over the previous five years at bank statements, IRS records, or Social Security records, and if they have questions, they allow applicants only 10 days to answer those questions. It can often be difficult to pull the necessary records together. Just completing the actual Medicaid application can be pretty daunting, but when all of these other things are added, the process can be extra challenging.

Given all of the issues and the difficulties of navigating the Medicaid maze, a lot of people work with elder law attorneys to help them through the process and, at the same time, protect their resources. The sooner you start planning for these long-term, nursing-home-care costs, and planning for Medicaid, the more options you will have available, mainly because of that five-year look-back period. It is important to start thinking about this and planning for this before you need nursing home care so that you can put together some proactive solutions.

There are many myths and truths about Medicaid planning. Myth number one is the belief that if your spouse or you go into a nursing home or need long-term care at home or in an assisted living facility, the state will take away your home. Well, the truth is, the home is an exempt asset, assuming that you intend to return to it. The legal planning we do at my firm always assumes that the person that we plan for intends to live at home.

If a spouse lives at home, or a disabled child lives at home, steps can be taken to protect it. We also need to be concerned about estate recovery, but there are legal strategies, including a legacy deed or asset protection trust, which can be used to protect the home. The truth is that the house can be protected even if you go on to Medicaid if you take the legal steps necessary to do so.

The second myth is the belief that if you give assets away, you have to wait 36 months to qualify for Medicaid. The truth is that the look-back period now is 60 months under the new law that went into effect in 2007. Also, the 60-month period is only a look-back period. You would face a divestment penalty, but you would not automatically be disqualified for Medicaid.

The third myth is the belief that if you are already in a nursing home, it is too late to shelter any assets. The truth is that it is never too late to plan. We have what we call planning clients and crisis clients. Planning clients plan ahead with the idea that they are not going to set foot in a nursing home within the next year, couple of years, or even five years or longer. We have a lot of options for them, and we can usually protect the majority, if not all, of their assets. However, even if the loved one is already in a nursing home, there are things that an elder care attorney can do to protect a substantial amount of his or her assets.

Myth number four is the belief that you can give away $14,000 a year without any type of penalty. The truth is that taxes and the way the IRS works is completely different from the way Medicaid works. For Medicaid purposes, there is no *de minimis* tax rule, which means there is no minimum in terms of the amount you are allowed to gift. Even if you give away $50 to little Johnny on his birthday, theoretically, a caseworker could say that is a divestment.

The fifth myth is the belief that all you have to do to protect your assets is to purchase an annuity. The truth is that annuities often are oversold by insurance professionals. They may be a planning tool, but, if not used properly, they can severely limit planning options and the amount of assets that can be protected.

The final myth is the belief that you do not need to plan for long-term care because there is only a small chance that you will ever end up in a nursing home anyway. The truth is one in two people over the age of 65 will spend some time in a nursing home. And that statistic is specific to nursing homes. It does not take home care or assisted living into account.

A big mistake we see people making time and time again is believing it is too late to plan. It is never too late to start planning for nursing home costs. Even if you have already set foot in a nursing home, we can generally put together a plan to protect some of your resources.

Another mistake we see people making is giving away their assets in an inefficient manner. For example, if you are just giving assets outright to children, what happens if they spend those assets? You also have gift tax issues. What happens if the person you have given those assets to were to get a divorce or get involved in a lawsuit? Generally, working within an asset protection trust is a better way to protect those resources.

Many people completely fail to plan for estate recovery. In other words, they fail to protect the house after the Medicaid applicant has passed away. The Medicaid process is a complex maze with a bunch of rules that do not always make sense. A lot of misinformation comes from friends and family or people who have gone through the process but have experienced a slightly different situation. There are a lot of potholes, so it is important to talk to an expert in the area to properly plan for nursing home Medicaid assistance.

As I mentioned earlier, in the case of Bill and Judy, after we set up veterans' benefits for both of them, a number of years passed. Bill continued to receive care at home until he needed to transition to assisted living with memory care. The VA benefit continued paying $2,054 a month. It helped Judy continue to live and have a certain quality of life while still paying for Bill's care, even as he entered assisted living and then transitioned into assisted living with memory care. After six years, because his health declined, Bill needed 24/7 skilled care. At this point he entered a local nursing home.

The great thing was that when he entered the nursing home, because of the planning we had done six years earlier, he was able to immediately qualify for Medicaid, even though, normally, Bill and Judy's assets would have been above the Medicaid asset limit. By taking legal steps within the Medicaid rules, Bill and Judy protected their life savings from nursing home spend-down.

Because of the special type of asset protection trust we established, they were able to receive immediate qualification and did not have to pay the $10,000-a-month nursing home bill that normally would have been due and would have drained Judy's assets. What this meant for Judy is that she had the peace of mind to afford to pay for the best care possible for her husband and ensure that she wouldn't be impoverished herself, thereby protecting her quality of life.

At the end of the day, Judy had the peace of mind to know that even though Bill's long-term-care costs were extraordinarily high, she would be legally protected from having to pay them, and she could rest easy, knowing that she could continue to have a good quality of life, even as Bill received the care he needed.

Of course, not everyone plans ahead as Bill and Judy did. In that same situation, if a husband entered a nursing home without doing any type of planning, the family could be on the hook for $10,000 or $11,000 a month in nursing home costs. But there are also options available when we are in what we call "crisis planning," when no planning has taken place before someone enters a nursing home. Let's look at the example of Matt and Rose.

Matt is suffering from Parkinson's. While Rose is still living relatively healthy, Matt enters a nursing home and Rose comes into our office because she has been referred by a social worker at the nursing home. She is concerned about long-term-care costs. Matt and Rose have $200,000 worth of countable resources. Rose is concerned that if she is paying $10,000 a month for Matt's care, she will not have anything to live on moving forward. They have not done any type of planning other than creating powers of attorney and a will.

Rose's options are that she could pay $10,000 a month until she is basically impoverished (not a good option), or she could put together a Medicaid plan whereby nearly 100 percent of her assets would be protected from long-term-care costs. This is what we did, using a specialized type of trust called "a sole benefit trust." It stipulated that as long as Rose was healthy and living in the community while Matt received care in a 24/7 skilled nursing home, we could funnel the assets to Rose so she would not be impoverished.

The only thing she would lose would be the patient pay amount, which would be Matt's income to the nursing home every month. This came from his Social Security benefits and pension, which, in this case, was only $2,000. Matt and Rose would pay $2,000 a month to the nursing home versus the $10,000 a month they would have had to pay had we not set up a sole benefit trust. It gave Rose the peace of mind to know that, moving forward, she would be able to maintain her quality of life.

That is what we can do for a married couple. It is different for a widow or a single individual. Let's look at Julie's case. Julie is in a nursing home suffering from multiple sclerosis and she has been there for six months. Her son and daughter are concerned about the high cost of care and they are running out of assets. Julie has only $150,000 worth of assets and a house, and they want to obtain additional services for her, but they do not want the money to run out. They understand that when the money runs out, so do the options. The more options you have, generally, the better quality of life you have.

In Julie's case, we were able to protect some of the resources. We used a specialized type of legal plan whereby we could protect roughly half of the assets. The plan allowed half of the assets to be used for the costs associated with a single individual in a nursing home, and the remainder of the assets to be protected and used to pay for additional services if necessary. Also, if the nursing home patient were to pass away, those assets could be passed down to the next generation.

We were able to protect her liquid assets, and we were able to protect her house from estate recovery. If the state pays any costs of care, say through Medicaid, it can potentially place a lien on a house. The lien would have to be paid off before the next generation would be able to do anything, including selling the house. By using a specialized type of deed called a legacy deed, we were able to maintain that exemption from Medicaid during Julie's lifetime, but also avoid the estate recovery when she passed away.

The net effect was that we were able to protect more than half of the liquid assets, as well as the family home, versus the alternative in which Julie would have just paid the nursing home every month until she was left with only $2,000. On top of that, the state would come in after she passed away to take away the home. Julie's family was very happy that they had sat down with a Certified Elder Law Attorney to review their options.

The key is to try to plan ahead as early as possible, but I understand that many people do not do this. Even if you do not plan ahead and are operating from a crisis standpoint, there are still options available. But planning ahead is always—always—the best course of action.

Hospice

The term *hospice* refers to the palliative care of a terminally ill patient with roughly six months or less to live. It is not necessarily a death sentence. Palliative care is specialized medical care for people with serious illnesses. It is focused on providing patients with relief from the symptoms, pain, and stress of a serious illness, whatever the prognosis. The goal is to improve quality of life for both the patient and family members, who are the central system for care.

A patient can live at a hospice house or receive in-home hospice care for a number of years. But, generally, for someone to qualify for hospice care, a doctor has to diagnose that patient as terminally sick with only a short time left to live.

Once the doctor makes that determination, the patient's family can choose to receive hospice care services, which are much less focused on helping a patient recover than managing that patient's pain and quality of life. Typically, hospice services are covered by Medicare as well as some health insurance providers. Hospice care is also sometimes covered through a nonprofit organization.

At my firm we believe doctors don't talk to patients enough about hospice care. Too often doctors are only interested in treating patients for their illness, even when there may not be any real chance for recovery. So, while doctors are hesitant to recommend or refer patients to hospice, it is important for families to understand when a loved one could quality for hospice.

Medicare pays for hospice care, but this is only one of the ways we can pay for hospice care. There are also a number of nonprofits that provide a hospice system. Among the main hospice services are helping the patient die with dignity and easing that transition.

One of the keys to trigger Medicare for hospice is a referral from a doctor. As I mentioned, doctors are often hesitant to bring the subject up. Sometimes it is up to a social worker, or someone else who is familiar with hospice care, to bring the subject to a doctor's attention.

Hospice services can be delivered in the home, or at an assisted living facility, nursing home, veterans' facility or a hospital. A group of hospice providers, including nurses and chaplains, make sure the hospice patient is comfortable. Most hospice care is delivered at home because that is where people are most comfortable. Everyone wants to be in the least restrictive, most comfortable setting possible.

Generally, a hospital is not going to be the most comfortable setting. A client I talked with today has spent the last year taking his wife in and out of hospitals. She has suffered from a variety of ailments but now has a urinary tract infection. They have gotten to the point where they are now going to speak with the doctors about hospice care. They won't have to bounce back and forth between the hospital and home. She will remain at home. Hospice care staff will come in to make sure that her transition is as comfortable as possible.

Hospice care started as more of a volunteer-like movement, but these days, a lot of nonprofits still provide hospice care, even though Medicare dollars now come into play. Many times, after caring for a patient, a nonprofit hospice service will ask for a donation to its cause. If the family feels that the hospice service was helpful, a donation is an appropriate gesture.

From a legal perspective, once loved ones are on hospice care, it becomes very important to ensure that their legal affairs are in order before they pass away.

When a loved one has passed away, we deal with what is called estate administration. In reality, there are about four ways in which assets are transferred from a loved one's name upon death. The first is through joint ownership. Many married couples' assets are in joint ownership, whereby if the husband passes away, say, the house will go to the wife outright.

The second way assets can be transferred is through beneficiary designations. If you have a life insurance policy and you have named a beneficiary, if you were to pass away, the benefit would go to the person named as your beneficiary.

The third way is through a trust. A lot of people have revocable living trusts, with beneficiaries named in that trust.

If an asset does not pass through one of these three ways, it ends up going through probate, which, as we have seen, is a court process that can take five months to a year and eat up generally 3 to 5 percent of any of the assets that pass through probate.

The last will and testament is a tricky thing. As we have seen, a lot of people think that a will avoids probate, but in reality, a will just gives instructions to the probate court on how to administer someone's estate. When a loved one passes away, it is important that the assets be appropriately transferred out of the loved one's name and that this transaction is handled through estate administration.

Legal Strategies

There are many important legal strategies that you must consider when planning for a loved one with a chronic illness. This chapter will discuss many of those legal strategies, but it is not exhaustive because the legal environment, laws, governmental agencies, and benefits are always changing. The best advice I can offer is to get the help of an elder law attorney or Certified Elder Law Attorney in your area.

With that said, I want to share with you some foundational planning that has held true for many years. Some of this may be a review of previous chapters, but it is important for me to drill home these concepts, because they can be complex and confusing at times.

One of the first things we look at when families come into our office is a financial power of attorney. Often, a financial power of attorney document is drafted from an estate planning perspective versus an elder law perspective. An estate planning perspective would be focused on what happens when you pass away. An elder law perspective is more concerned about what happens if you do not pass away and continue to age. A financial power of attorney document drafted from an elder law perspective is going to take into consideration planning for veterans' benefits, or planning for Medicaid, or planning for what happens if you are diagnosed with Alzheimer's or dementia and you lose your ability to function.

That is the starting point for any type of elder law planning: making sure that you have a financial power of attorney drafted from an elder law perspective, where there may be fewer limitations on gifts. There may be, specifically, the ability to set up trusts on behalf of the person who has created the financial power of attorney. The financial power of attorney document may specify the ability to maneuver assets for Medicaid benefits or maneuver assets for veterans' benefits. But a typical financial power of attorney document does not allow for that type of thing. It is important to have a well-drafted financial power of attorney document with an elder law focus. That is the starting point.

From there it will depend on the client's goals and what the client is trying to protect against. At our firm we plan for our clients on a couple of different levels, beginning with standard estate planning, whereby we make sure that our clients' possessions will go to their loved ones in the way they want them to go. We create financial powers of attorney and medical powers of attorney, as well as trust documents and wills.

If clients are interested in protecting their assets against long-term-care costs, we might talk about setting up an asset protection trust. The purpose of that asset protection trust would be to protect against Medicaid spend-down. If a client's spouse or surviving spouse were a veteran, an asset protection trust would help that spouse qualify for VA benefits.

Elder law is more than just planning for what happens if the client passes away, which is what estate planning focuses on. Elder law also involves planning for what happens if the client does not pass away. Elder law attorneys look at the types of assets the client owns, including retirement accounts, life insurance, and real estate, and that is all tied together and incorporated into the necessary legal documents. For example, if the client has a house, one of the things we might create is a legacy deed to protect the house against estate recovery. If the client is focusing on protection-type planning to protect against long-term-care costs and has an asset protection trust, we may put the deed directly into the asset protection trust.

There are a couple of types of asset protection trusts we can create, depending on whether the client is a veteran or not, or whether we are only concerned with Medicaid planning. If the client is a veteran, we use what is called a veterans' asset protection trust, into which the client can put assets, using the trust as a piggy bank. Clients have to name someone other than themselves as the trustee, but the veterans' asset protection trust immediately qualifies them for VA benefits.

In contrast, the goal of a Medicaid asset protection trust is to start the five-year clock ticking for Medicaid purposes. A Medicaid asset protection trust affords a little more flexibility and allows the person who created the trust to also be the trustee. In addition, it allows for more control over where the income generated from the trust assets goes. For example, the income that is generated from the veterans' asset protection trust cannot go back to the veteran because that could disqualify him or her for VA benefits. The income from the Medicaid asset protection trust, on the other hand, can flow back to the owner of the trust.

One of the important goals for many of our clients is to protect the family home, and there are a couple of ways we can do that. The first involves using what is called a legacy deed, whereby the deed is in the name of the original owners while they are alive and, when they pass away, can go to the revocable trust, the kids, or whichever beneficiary the owners want, thereby avoiding probate and avoiding estate recovery.

Another option would be to place the house in an asset protection trust to start that five-year clock ticking on the Medicaid look-back period so that if the person who created the trust can make it five years without needing nursing home care and paying its costs, the house would be exempt from Medicaid claims on it.

Another of my cases concerned Ruth, who was the widow of a veteran. She lived at home, but one of her daughters provided care for her.

In Ruth's case, the legal strategies we used included putting together a veterans' asset protection trust to help Ruth qualify for the VA benefit. We approached Ruth's case from an asset standpoint because she had more than $400,000 worth of assets. She was not paying any money out of pocket to caregivers, even though one of her daughters was taking time off work to help provide care for her.

As part of the legal strategy, we put together a care contract for Ruth so that she could pay her daughter roughly $1,500 per month. The daughter was living with Ruth 24/7. A commercial home care company could easily have cost Ruth up to $15,000 a month. Ruth was getting quite the deal from her daughter, and all we were doing was documenting the $1,500 going from Ruth to her daughter. That qualified Ruth on the income test for veterans' benefits as well. Because Ruth's husband served 90 days of active duty, one day during a period of war, and he was not dishonorably discharged, Ruth could meet all the other requirements of the VA benefit.

Now that she was paying her daughter $1,500 a month, Ruth was able to bring in an additional $1,113 a month, tax-free, from the VA to pay for additional services and further protect her resources against future long-term-care costs.

Also, because Ruth was living in her own house, we were concerned about estate recovery. We wanted to make sure that her estate would avoid probate, so we deeded her house into the asset protection trust as well. We knew that, at some future date, home care might be insufficient for Ruth, who could then transition to an assisted living community. At that point the house would provide no real benefit to her and could be an asset we could later sell to provide for additional care and services for Ruth. Because the house was in the asset protection trust, when it was sold, Ruth was not disqualified from the governmental benefit she was receiving. That was the legal strategy we used for Ruth, who was a widow/surviving veteran. Luckily, the family came in right when Ruth started to need care.

Now, not everyone plans ahead. For example, Rose was a widow, but she was not a veteran. Her son came into our office because Rose had entered a nursing home with advanced Alzheimer's and needed the medical care provided by a 24/7 skilled community. She had not done any planning but did have roughly $150,000. Her son was concerned because they were paying out $10,000 a month for her care. Rose understood that when she ran out of money, she would run out of options.

Even though Rose had done no planning as Ruth had, we were able to put together a legal plan to protect roughly half of her assets, using a strategy called half-load planning. In that strategy we were able to protect half of the assets so that they could be used for additional services for Rose. The other half of her assets, roughly $75,000, had to be spent on nursing home care. Instead of spending the entire $150,000 on nursing home care and running out of money in 15 months, Rose was able to qualify for Medicaid in about eight months, with roughly $75,000 protected for additional services.

When you are on Medicaid, you are able to keep only $60 worth of income per month. For Rose, that equated only to a haircut each month. Now, her son has $75,000 for additional services for her. A nursing home is not a jail sentence; you are still entitled to quality of life.

Through the entire long-term-care journey, there are many opportunities to protect and improve quality of life, as well as many potholes that can completely eat up all of a family's hard-earned assets and resources. Once those resources are gone, so are many of a family's options and choices. It's my job, as a Certified Elder Law Attorney, to protect the quality of life of those who need costly health care. The legal strategies that I've shared in this book are the tools I use to do that.

Bill and Judy Revisited

T o recap, Judy came into my office. She was about 10 years younger than her husband, Bill, who was a 65-year-old veteran, suffering from Alzheimer's. Judy, his caregiver, was concerned about long-term-care costs and how she would live if she were to pay his long-term-care costs out of her own pocket. She had a long life expectancy and was very concerned that Bill should be well taken care of and that she would have money left over at the end of the day.

What we put in place for Bill and Judy was a veterans' asset protection trust so we could help Bill immediately qualify for VA benefits because he was entering an assisted living community. To get Bill and Judy's assets under the VA asset limits, we put their house in the trust so we could protect it. If they needed to sell the house in the future, the proceeds from the sale would be protected as well.

We put together and submitted the VA application once we had the trust funded for Bill and Judy. It took six to eight months to become approved, after which Judy received a lump sum of more than $12,000 in her account. These funds were intended to help her cover the cost of care for Bill, who was now in an assisted living community. She then received $2,054 a month for a number of years while Bill lived in the assisted living community. Eventually, he fell and broke his hip. Because he was not healthy enough to remain at the assisted living community, he had to transition to a nursing home.

The nursing home cost was $10,000 a month, and the VA benefit maxed out at $2,054 a month. At that time, instead of relying on the VA benefits to help pay the cost of care for Bill, we relied on the Medicaid program. Because we had created a veterans' asset protection trust five years earlier, the assets that were held in trust did not have to be spent down on any type of Medicaid spend-down program, and we were able to immediately qualify Bill for Medicaid in the nursing home. Judy was able to protect all of her assets and resources to provide income that was over and above what Medicaid provided for Bill. When Bill finally passed away, the couple's estate avoided probate and was available to Judy for her use on her own care.

That is what we did for Bill and Judy. We can find the right solution for you too. One of the most important things to do for the elder care journey and the care of a loved one who may be suffering from a chronic illness is to plan. This obviously holds true even for people not suffering from a chronic illness, because the earlier you plan, the more options you have. The more options you have, generally, the better results you have, and better results mean better quality of life.

It is important to seek out a Certified Elder Law Attorney to explore the options available to you as you go on your elder care journey. It is important to protect yourself against long-term-care costs. In the past, attorneys were only concerned with avoiding estate taxes, which are not an issue today unless you have more than $5 million. What people are more concerned about these days is avoiding long-term-care costs, which can easily run to more than $10,000 a month. If you have a concern about protecting your resources against long-term care, or questions on how to care for a loved one suffering from a chronic illness, it is important to seek out a Certified Elder Law Attorney.

CONCLUSION

Picking up the phone to call an attorney can be stressful and, often, when a client sits down with an attorney, it is the first time that client has worked with an attorney. So the experience can be pretty scary.

Generally, people call because they are concerned about future long-term-care costs and planning for a loved one's care. We usually get calls from the caregivers, who invest their emotions, finances, and time to care for their loved ones. They want to make sure they are taking the correct steps. Unfortunately, in elder-care planning and long-term-care planning, a lot of mistakes can be made because the rules are confusing.

Our role as elder care attorneys is to help clients navigate that long-term-care legal maze on that elder care journey. What we find is that people generally start off pretty healthy, but as they continue to age and face some of the issues that go along with aging—chronic illnesses such as Alzheimer's, dementia, and Parkinson's—they begin to suffer from an increasingly limited ability to function and, as a consequence, need more care. They begin to lose some of their independence.

Most people want to live at home as long as possible and it is important to have a plan for that, but they may get to a point where that is not an option anymore and they must bring in home care. Home care may come from family members—from a spouse, or a son or a daughter.

Sometimes, living at home, even with the help of commercial home care, is no longer feasible. When the chronically ill senior needs a more protective environment, many times, he or she will transition to an assisted living community or independent living community. If the senior has memory issues, he or she may transition to an assisted living community with memory care.

The final stop, as that senior's ability to function continues to diminish and more assistance with daily living activities is needed, is a 24/7 skilled nursing community.

It is important to understand that these different levels of care entail widely varying costs. Generally, home care companies are going to charge $1,000 to $3,000 a month for a couple of hours of service per day, a couple of times per week. For 24/7 skilled care, the cost easily could be $15,000.

Assisted living community costs might run between $2,000 and $5,000 a month. Assisted living with memory care might run from $5,000 to $7,000 month. Skilled nursing may run from $7,000 to $11,000 a month. These numbers can be eye opening for caregivers and seniors who are concerned about long-term-care costs.

Unfortunately, the system is broken in the sense that insurance policies pay for surgery after a heart attack, which can easily cost

$500,000 to $1 million. Yet, we do not have a great system set up to pay for long-term-care costs. That is where a Certified Elder Law Attorney comes in to try to balance the scales in favor of those needing long-term care.

The system is set up against both the caregiver and the senior who needs care. We have only six ways to pay for long-term-care costs. It is our job as Certified Elder Law Attorneys to guide clients through them. There is no magic wand or magic bullet to pay for long-term-care costs. You can private pay—pay out of your own funds—or you can have your kids pick up the bill. But who wants to have their kids pay their long-term-care costs?

A third way is Medicare. Some people think Medicare is going to pay the entire cost of care, but we know that Medicare pays only for short-term rehab. Then we have long-term-care insurance, which is fraught with issues, and not a lot of people have it anyway. Even those who do sometimes do not understand exactly what they have.

Then we have the VA, which is an amazing program for veterans and surviving spouses. It helps pay for home care or assisted living. When you pay $7,000 to $11,000 a month for nursing home costs, you need to transition to a different governmental program. That one is called Medicaid.

Unfortunately, these governmental programs have different rules that sometimes butt heads. It is important that you have a trusted guide, an experienced Certified Elder Law Attorney, to guide you through this long-term-care maze. It is not just about protecting your money. It is about having options and improving your loved one's quality of life. If you are putting in time as a caregiver, you want to make sure that you are taking the right steps and giving that person the best options, the best quality of life possible. That is why it is *essential* to work with a Certified Elder Law Attorney.

For more information, visit www.TheElderCareFirm.com.

31901056941281

CPSIA information can be obtained at www.ICGtesting.com
Printed in the USA
BVOW05s1400280216

438382BV00024B/208/P